WHEN
KIDS
GET
ARRESTED

WHEN
KIDS
GET
ARRESTED

What Every Adult Should Know

Sandra Simkins

RUTGERS UNIVERSITY PRESS
NEW BRUNSWICK, NEW JERSEY, AND LONDON

Library of Congress Cataloging-in-Publication Data

Simkins, Sandra 1965–

When kids get arrested : what every adult should know / Sandra Simkins.

p. cm.

Includes bibliographical references and index.

ISBN 978-0-8135-4638-4 (hardcover : alk. paper) —

ISBN 978-0-8135-4639-1 (pbk. : alk. paper)

1. Juvenile justice, Administration of—United States.   I. Title.

KF9779.S54 2009

345.73'08—dc22

2009000782

A British Cataloging-in-Publication record for this book is available from the British Library.

Visit our Web site: http://rutgerspress.rutgers.edu

Manufactured in the United States of America

To
Steve,
Elizabeth,
AND
Grace

Contents

Figures and Tables

FIGURES

TABLES

Acknowledgments

I would like to thank the following people for their support and assistance throughout this process: Beverly Beaver, Marty Beyer, Jane Broder, Laurel Budman, Sue Burell, Barbara Dundon, Jocelyn Fowler, Marni Gangle, Lili Garfinkle, Lisa Geis, Mark Houldin, Sara Jacobson, Gwenn Jones, Marsha Levick, Robert Listenbee, National Juvenile Defender Center, Nicole Pittman, Ronnie Polaneczky, Patti Puritz, Denise Ray, Sarah Ricks, Lourdes Rosado, Mary Ann Scali, Meredith Schalick, Riya Shah, Fran Sherman, Karl and Alberta Simkins, Susan Simkins, Abbe Smith, Rebecca Starr, Joe Tulman, Marlie Wasserman, Robert Williams, and Leni Windle.

If you only have five minutes. . . .

1. Don't ever allow the police to question a child without a lawyer present.
2. Don't ever encourage a child to waive the right to a lawyer.
3. Juvenile records count: they do not disappear when a child turns eighteen.
4. Make sure you understand how the juvenile court deal will follow the child into the future. There are many long-term hidden consequences of juvenile court involvement. (See chapter 7.)
5. Children who get probation have not "beaten" the case. Assist your child in completing all the terms of probation as quickly as possible. And make sure you pay off all the restitution.
6. Be *really* worried if:
   a. The child is being sent to adult court—adult prison is not good for children.
   b. The child is charged with any type of sexual offense—a child labeled a sexual offender may be subject to lifetime registration and civil commitment.
7. Stay in touch with children who are sent to a residential placement and ask questions to make sure they are safe.
8. Race matters: minority children are treated more harshly at every stage of the juvenile court process.
9. Avoid the juvenile justice system if you can—it has become much more punitive since the mid-1990s and is rarely a good solution to school problems, mental health issues, or a defiant daughter.
10. Talk to your child(ren) in advance about what to do in case they are stopped by police. Have your child(ren) carry a copy of the "nonwaiver of rights" form (page 18) for additional protection.

WHEN
KIDS
GET
ARRESTED

Introduction

No one is ever prepared for the arrest of a child. Unlike a medical emergency, when it comes to a legal crisis in delinquency court, people don't know where to go for help. As a juvenile defense attorney, I've watched confused adults face the maze of juvenile court and unknowingly make choices that will dramatically alter the life course of a child they care about. Unfortunately, these choices are made in a vacuum of isolation, embarrassment, and misinformation.

For years I have been on the other end of the phone with someone encountering the juvenile justice system for the first time. I get calls from social workers, teachers, and coaches: the confusion is always the same. Sometimes they call when the child has just been arrested and is sitting down at the police station. Sometimes they call when a warrant has been issued for the child's arrest, and they have an hour to turn the child into police custody. Sometimes parents are so exhausted by their child's behavior they are ready to call the police themselves. The first thing I say is "You've done the right thing by asking for help."

This book is intended to help those who care about children understand the juvenile court process. I sometimes refer to "parents," but the guidance will be equally valuable to all those who have contact with children who become caught in the juvenile justice system. At the beginning of each chapter I highlight the top few tips I believe are most important at that stage. The reality is that two children, arrested for the same thing, can have completely different outcomes. The difference depends on how the case is handled. Most adults, if educated, can help the child make better choices.

No longer is juvenile court a place where you get a clean slate when you turn eighteen. Today almost every adjudication of delinquency is accompanied by long-term consequences, including DNA tests and adult-style fingerprinting.

Regardless of what kind of crime the child has been arrested for, there are certain basic legal concepts adults should know. This book is written from the position of a defense attorney. I want you to know what you can do to minimize the impact of the arrest on the child's life. The juvenile justice system has become much more punitive in the last fifteen years, and because of that, adults need to understand the long-range consequences of their decisions.

Most adults have no idea that juvenile court involvement can bring such damaging consequences, and instead they make choices that will "get the case over fast." Standing in the courthouse, under the pressure of the child's court date, unknowing guardians are vulnerable to information from the following biased sources:

- Police officers who pretend to be on the child's side, taking an incriminating statement and giving that statement to the prosecutor.
- The court sheriff or crier, whose main job is to keep the court docket moving.
- The prosecutor, whose job it is to keep the community safe and who may have a career interest in having the child admit to the most serious charge.
- The judge who encourages parents to give up their child's right to an attorney for the sake of expediency, or because "it's only probation," or because "the child needs help."

Over and over adults are encouraged to "go with the flow" and give up important legal rights that were designed to protect children. These legal rights, once given up, can not be reclaimed. What appears to be a good deal at the beginning can become a nightmare in the end.

This book is not intended to take the place of an attorney. The U.S. Supreme Court entitles children to have an attorney represent them in juvenile court, and concerned adults should be certain to work with the child's lawyer. Rather, this book is intended to give adults information in plain language to help them work more effectively with the child's attorney and understand the consequences of their choices. This book is not intended to answer the specific questions of every local jurisdiction; however, for specific issues I break down information by state.

So, let me be your guide. Once you understand how the system works, you will be a great advocate. If, after reading this, you need more information, the resource guide in the back will point you in the right direction.

PART I

The Juvenile Justice Process

1

Overview of Juvenile Court

> **TOP TIPS**
> 1. Children who have been arrested are entitled to important legal rights. The most important of these rights is the right to an attorney.
> 2. Children should NEVER give up (waive) their right to have a lawyer.
> 3. Children are different from adults: their brains are still developing and they may not be able to think like adults.

ALWAYS WORK WITH AN ATTORNEY

Trying to navigate the juvenile justice system without a lawyer is like trying to be your own doctor. You might be able to do it, but it is definitely not smart. Ever since Gerald Gault got sentenced to six years for making a prank phone call, children who get arrested have been entitled to important legal protections.[1] The most important of these rights is the right to be represented by a lawyer, even if you cannot afford one.

Unfortunately, although the *Gault* case secured legal rights for children, many well-meaning adults encourage children to waive these important rights. Of the approximately 2.1 million children who get arrested each year, in some parts of the country as many as 80 to 90 percent waive their right to counsel.[2] Waiving the right to an attorney is telling the court you don't want the help of a lawyer. This is crazy! Waiving your right to legal counsel denies you the expertise of a trained professional who will focus *specifically* on the child's case and give advice about potential outcomes.

So, why do so many concerned adults encourage children to waive the right to a lawyer? In my experience, the explanation for refusing a lawyer falls into one of three categories:

- I don't have time: usually stated as "I just want this to be over with" or "I've got to get back to work."
- Juvenile court is no big deal: most frequently stated as "my brother-in-law (or the security guard outside, or the sheriff, or the prosecutor) told me that it is best if my kid just admits to the charges."
- I don't need a lawyer because my child "did it."

None of these reasons makes any sense.

I Don't Have Time for This

First, I understand that your work is very important. However, if you are going to miss work for something, this is an extremely good reason. The juvenile court system is not something to rush through. Slow down and make sure you understand everything that is happening to the child.

Juvenile court may require several court appearances. When you take the time to work with a lawyer, your case may move more slowly. Remember, however, that admitting guilt gives your child the label of "juvenile delinquent." This negative label may follow the child far into the future. Why rush into it? Make sure the state has a real case against your child. Make sure you understand the consequences. At any point in the process you can always admit to the charges. That option never goes away. It may seem to you that when you go to juvenile court all you do is wait around and nothing happens. Even if it appears as though nothing is happening, it is still very important that the child is with a responsible adult at all times.

If you are concerned that missing work will cause you to lose your job, try to find an alternative adult to accompany the child. A family member is preferred, but a teacher or religious figure or coach will also substitute well.

This Is No Big Deal—My Brother-in-Law Told Me So

First, being found guilty in juvenile court is a big deal. Having a juvenile record can have a big impact on the child's future.

Secondly, not to disparage your relative, but consider the source. What legal expertise or bias/motive might the individual have? Does the prosecutor need a conviction to advance her career? Does the sheriff want to get home quickly so she can get to her second job? Gathering information is good, but be very selective about who you take advice from when it comes to a child's juvenile case.

I Don't Need a Lawyer: My Kid "Did It"

Think for a second about all the children of celebrities who get arrested in Hollywood for doing something stupid. Did they do it? Probably. Do they go to court without lawyers? Of course not. Celebrities want to get the best outcome possible for their children, and they won't be able to get that without a lawyer.

Even if the child "did it" and wants to admit to the charges, there are still so many things a lawyer can do to assist the child. Juvenile court is not simple. There are many hidden consequences that can follow a child into the future.

Since the 1990s, juvenile courts have become much more punitive. It used to be that no matter what a child did as a juvenile, when he reached eighteen, the child would have a clean record. Most adults still believe that if something happens when you are a juvenile it "won't count" when you become an adult. Let me be clear. It counts. In the 1990s almost every state revised its juvenile code. There was fear about "superpredators" and many politicians scored points with a "get tough on juvenile crime platform."

In this age of technology, information is easily accessible. Data on juvenile records is kept by every state and police department. It is easy to track a child by date of birth and social security number. Very few juveniles actually go through the process of getting an expungement (the legal proceeding to erase criminal records), so these juvenile records continue to pop up every time a person applies for a job. Some of the long-term consequences are laid out in chapter 7, but be aware that being found guilty in juvenile court can impact the following:

- Immigration
- Public housing
- School
- Getting into the military
- Sex offender registration

Working with a lawyer provides an opportunity to minimize the impact of the case on the child's life today, and to minimize the impact of the case on the child's future.

WHAT LEGAL RIGHTS DO CHILDREN HAVE?

In addition to the right to an attorney, children who get arrested have the following due process rights:

- The privilege against self-incrimination (you *do not* have to give a statement when questioned by police, and police *are* allowed to lie to you to get you to give a statement)
- The right to confront and cross-examine witnesses
- The right to be notified of the charges
- The right to a transcript of court proceedings
- The right to appeal
- The right to proof beyond a reasonable doubt

WHAT RIGHTS DON'T CHILDREN HAVE?

In most states children do not have the right to bail or the right to a trial by jury. (See chapter 3 for a list of which states afford children the right to bail and chapter 6 for a list of which states allow children the right to a jury trial.) However, regardless of what state you are in, if your child's case is transferred to adult criminal court, your child will have the right to a jury trial.

HOW LONG CAN A CHILD STAY IN
THE JUVENILE JUSTICE SYSTEM?

In most states, if an arrest occurs before a child's eighteenth birthday, she will be in juvenile court. If the child gets arrested on her eighteenth birthday, she will be in the adult criminal system. However, juvenile court doesn't end when a child turns eighteen. In most states juvenile court jurisdiction can last up to age twenty-one, and in some states, juvenile courts can have jurisdiction through age twenty-four.

WHY IS MY KID MAKING SUCH BAD CHOICES? ADOLESCENT DEVELOPMENT BASICS

There is a reason that teens make adults crazy. Recent brain research reveals that teens are often poor decision makers because their brains are not sufficiently developed. The part of the brain that is responsible for higher-level thinking and controlling impulses is not completely formed until a person is in his twenties. Stressful situations make things worse. Try to remember the following the next time you want to strangle your child.

- The teen brain is still developing.
- Young adults are frequently incapable of thinking like adults.
- Teens have a difficult time with impulse control and good judgment.
- Adolescents by their very nature are risk takers.
- Teens are more susceptible than adults to peer pressure.
- Teens are present focused and have a difficult time predicting long-term consequences.
- Just because teens look physically mature doesn't mean they have the same cognitive abilities to understand information and make good decisions.
- The ability of teens to make good decisions decreases when stress or peer pressure is involved.

For decades, laws have reflected the reality that children are not the same as adults. Teens under eighteen cannot buy alcohol, cigarettes, or see X-rated (now known as NC-17) movies. They can't vote, get a tattoo, or form contracts. These laws were created to protect them from making bad choices.

HOW IS JUVENILE COURT DIFFERENT FROM
ADULT CRIMINAL COURT?

The Language of Juvenile Court Is Different

Because the original creators of juvenile court wanted to create a separate court that protected children as much as possible from the stigma of being criminalized, a new language was created. For example:

Children are not arrested for a crime; they are charged with a delinquent act.

Children do not have a criminal trial; they have an adjudicatory hearing.

Children do not plead guilty; they admit to the charges.

Children are not convicted; they are found delinquent.

Children are not sentenced; they receive a disposition at a disposition hearing.

The Goal of Juvenile Court Is Different

Although juvenile court shares many of the procedures of adult criminal court, the purposes of the two courts are very different. The purpose of adult criminal court is punishment. The purpose of juvenile court is rehabilitation. While juvenile courts today seek to protect the public and promote accountability, in every state the goal is still to rehabilitate the child.

"Rehabilitation" is a word that can have very broad implications. Regardless of what your child is arrested for, it is generally within the juvenile court's jurisdiction to address the needs of that child. Understanding this court goal you can then organize your efforts not only to help your child but also to assist the court in meeting that goal. The more a court sees a parent as a partner in this rehabilitation, the greater control and impact the parent can have.

I do want to add a word of caution, however. Although the goal is rehabilitation, it can be dangerous for parents to think the juvenile court system is a solution for all the problems in their family. While the system helps some children, there are serious risks as well. Research shows that involvement in juvenile court

FIGURE 1.1 How a Typical Case Proceeds

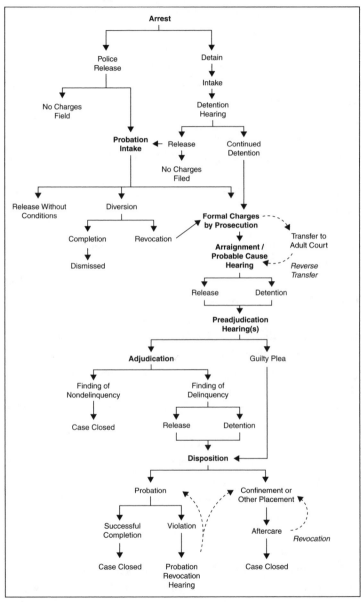

While jurisdictions may have different terms for particular stages of a case and/or slight variations in the order of proceedings, delinquency cases generally follow a basic structure. This book will address each of these stages, and the chart should aid you in visualizing the general flow of a case.

increases the likelihood that a child will subsequently be convicted and incarcerated as an adult.

Juvenile Courts Are
Overwhelmed with Cases

Juvenile courts across the country are overwhelmed. On any given day in 2004, juvenile courts handled approximately 4,500 delinquency cases. This kind of volume is hard to imagine unless you've seen it, but think piles and piles of files. Each file is filled with papers that could impact a child's life. This volume leads to pressure to move the court cases quickly. The more you can understand about juvenile court before you get there, the better off you will be.

Juvenile Court Is a Dumping Ground

Unfortunately, one of the reasons that juvenile courts are overwhelmed is because they have become a dumping ground for many children who have complex problems. The children who end up in juvenile court often have learning disabilities that have gone undiagnosed for years. I have frequently seen seventeen-year-olds with a second-grade reading level. Children come to juvenile court who have been abused or neglected, who have never gotten the trauma treatment they need to heal. They come to the court as a result of the fractured mental health system and suffer from serious mental disorders. Zero-tolerance policies in the schools and the war on drugs, which incarcerates so many parents, lead children to the juvenile justice system.

The courts are simply not able to handle such complex problems, particularly when there is such volume. My advice to adults is this: avoid the justice system if you can. If you have access to other services outside the system that could help your child (for example, your child has a drug problem and you have medical insurance that will pay for treatment), use them. While the goal of the juvenile court system is rehabilitation, it is still a criminal system. Avoid it if you can.

NOTES

1. *In re Gault*, 387 U.S. 358 (1967). The *Gault* case gives all children who are charged in delinquency court the right to an attorney. This 1967 case involved a fifteen-year-old Arizona boy who received a sentence of six years to a "training school for boys" after he was found guilty of making "lewd phone calls." Prior to 1967, children were not entitled to lawyers in delinquency court.

2. From National Juvenile Defender Center (NJDC) General Juvenile Justice facts and figures: 2.1 million, *OJJDP Statistical Briefing Book*, available online at: http://ojjdp.ncjrs .gov/ojstatbb/crime/qa05101.asp?qaData=2005. For 80 to 90 percent, from Judith B. Jones, *Access to Counsel, OJJDP Juvenile Justice Bulletin* (June 2004), available online at: http://www.ncjrs.org/pdffiles1/ojjdp/204063.pdf.

2

Interrogation
What the Police
Don't Want You to Know

FIGURE 2.1 Sample Nonwaiver of Rights Form

To the police and/or prosecutor

Please be advised that I do not wish to waive my right to remain silent. I also do not wish to speak without an attorney present

I wish to be represented by a lawyer.

- I DO NOT WISH TO SPEAK WITH YOU WITHOUT MY ATTORNEY PRESENT.
- I DO NOT CONSENT TO ANY SEARCH OF MY PERSON OR PROPERTY.
- I DO NOT CONSENT TO ANY LINEUP OR OTHER IDENTIFICATION PROCEDURE WITHOUT MY ATTORNEY.
- I WILL NOT WAIVE MY RIGHTS UNDER MIRANDA V. ARIZONA , WITHOUT THE PRESENCE OF MY ATTORNEY.

Date	Time	Name
		Attorney

My guardian/parent(s) name(s): _____

My address: _____

_____

My phone number: _____

My date of birth: _____

My attorney's name: _____

My attorney's phone number: _____

My attorney's registration number: _____

Source: Created by author, relying on *Miranda v. Arizona,* 384 U.S. 436 (1966).

During gym class, sixth-grader Darryl was playing basketball with his classmates. At one point, in the middle of the game, Darryl said "I'm going to kill you" to a child on the opposing team. The following day, the school called the police. The police took Darryl into a room alone, where he confessed to making the statement. Darryl was then taken to the police station and charged with terroristic threats. His statement was used by the prosecutor to find him guilty.

• • •

Twelve-year-old Carly was in a residential program for abused children. One day the police showed up and asked to talk to Carly about something that had happened eighteen months before. Nine-year-old Julia, who used to live with Carly in a group home, had recently told her social worker that Carly had touched her "private." Carly's case manager left her alone with the police, where she "confessed" to the crime. Carly was then charged as a sex offender and taken out of the program.

• • •

It was 7:00 P.M. when Carol heard the police knock on the door. Two uniformed officers explained that some homes in the neighborhood had been broken into and they thought her son Michael might have some information.

"Mind if we ask your son some questions?" the taller officer said.

"Well, I'm not sure," said Carol.

"It won't take long, and it could help Mike," said the second officer.

Carol let the officers in. After talking to the police a warrant was signed for Michael's arrest and his statement was used as the primary evidence against him.

• • •

The most important thing adults need to do at this stage is to prevent any police questioning without a lawyer. *Do not, under any circumstances, let your child give a statement to the police without an attorney present.* I can't emphasize this strongly enough. Over and over I have seen well-meaning adults encourage children to "tell the truth about what happened," only to see the child be convicted based on that statement. In most states it is completely legal for police to take statements from children (as young as ten years old) without an interested adult or attorney present. These statements *will* be used against the child at trial.

THEY DIDN'T READ ME MY RIGHTS!

Interrogation, or the questioning of your child by police, usually happens immediately after the arrest. However, because of the inaccuracy of most TV crime shows, confusion persists about being "read your rights." Most TV crime programs show the arrest and the reading of the rights as a simultaneous event. Generally, on TV, the moment the handcuffs are clicked the officer begins to say, "You have the right to remain silent, anything you say can and will be used against you." This works for TV, but in actuality, under the law the police only have to read someone his rights *if* they are going to take a statement from the person. If the police do not intend to take a statement from the person they have just arrested there is no reason for them to read her rights.

WHAT ARE MY RIGHTS?

"Reading your rights" comes from the Fifth Amendment to the U.S. Constitution and protects against self-incrimination. The Fifth Amendment states that "a citizen will never be compelled in any criminal case to be a witness against himself." The Fifth Amendment was further explained by the Supreme Court case of *Miranda v. Arizona*, 384 U.S. 436 (1966). *Miranda* held that if police intend to take a statement, they have to recite the following warnings to persons in custody:

- You have the right to remain silent.
- Anything you say can be used against you in court.
- You have the right to talk to a lawyer before we ask you any questions and to have your lawyer with you during questioning.
- If you cannot afford a lawyer, one will be appointed for you before questioning.
- If you decide to answer questions now without a lawyer present, you will still have the right to stop answering at any time until you talk to a lawyer.

WHY SHOULDN'T I LET MY CHILD GIVE A STATEMENT?
WON'T "TELLING THE TRUTH" HELP HIM?

What most adults don't understand is that children who are arrested can be questioned without having an attorney or an adult present. In many states it is totally permissible for a police office to question a child as young as ten without having any interested adult present. Once the child gives a statement, that statement can be used as evidence against the child.

The problem with children giving statements without an attorney present is that even though the child believes what he has to say will help him, it almost never does. The police are trained law enforcement officers. They are not neutral parties and it is not their job to help your child. They know exactly what crime the prosecution is trying to prove and what facts will help the prosecutor prove it. Police craft their questions in the interrogation to elicit statements they believe will be helpful in proving that the child did the crime. Otherwise why would the police have gone to the trouble of making the arrest?

Many children report that the officer said he would "go easy" on them if they gave a statement. Although I've handled thousands of cases and have dealt with hundreds of statements, I have never seen a police officer who took a statement from a child come to court to "help" the child, or ask the prosecutor to dismiss the charges.

Children think that if they were "just there" but didn't really do anything, it will be okay to say that. It's not. When a child says she was in the company of the codefendant, it makes the case more difficult to win. For example, in a car theft case, Jenny will give a statement that she watched Joey steal the car, but she never drove it. Or in a drug case, Richie will say, "I was only holding the money. I never made any sales myself." Or in a burglary case, Rakim will say, "I went in the house with him, but I didn't take anything." Each of these statements is enough to prove the child is guilty of something—maybe not the lead charge, but something—and these statements severely limit the child's trial options.

UNDERSTANDING THE LAW OF JUVENILE CONFESSIONS

Although the Supreme Court has cautioned that children need special protection, there is no longer a bright line rule that requires the presence of an interested adult. Children can be questioned alone even when the consequences are extreme.

The case of Anthony Harris provides a good example. Anthony Harris was twelve years old when his six-year-old neighbor, Devan, was murdered. Anthony had no prior involvement in the juvenile justice system. The police had absolutely no physical evidence that tied Anthony to the crime. However, the police department in the town of New Philadelphia, Ohio, called in an expert on interrogation, Chief Vaughn, to take a statement from Anthony.

First, Chief Vaughn lied to Anthony's mother when he told her that he was just taking Anthony down to the station for a "voice stress test." When Anthony's mom asked to be in the room with her son, she was told that "it would be better if you wait outside."

Next, while Anthony was in the room alone with the officer, Chief Vaughn read Anthony his rights, told him that he had the right to an attorney, then began to question him for an hour. The chief repeatedly made false statements about evidence he did not have in order to make Anthony think he would be found guilty of the murder.

Anthony made a statement confessing to murdering Devan. Since there was no other evidence connecting Anthony to the crime, his statement became the State's primary tool in the trial. At trial, Anthony was found guilty of murder.

Tactics that police use to interrogate children can vary widely across states. There is a 2004 case from Wisconsin of a fourteen-year-old boy whose intelligence was in the low range of normal. While the police questioned him, he was handcuffed to a wall and left alone for two hours. His request to call his parents was denied, and he was then questioned for five and a half hours before finally signing a written statement prepared by the detective.[1]

For a state-by-state overview of what protections children have when being interrogated by the police, see tables 2.1 and 2.2.

TABLE 2.1 Policing Questioning: High-Risk States

In these states, police can interrogate a child alone, without having a lawyer or interested adult present.	
Alabama	Mississippi
Alaska	Missouri
Arizona	Nebraska
Arkansas	Nevada
California	New Hampshire
Delaware	New York
District of Columbia	Ohio
Florida	Oregon
Georgia	Pennsylvania
Hawaii	Rhode Island
Idaho	South Carolina
Illinois	South Dakota
Kentucky	Tennessee
Louisiana	Texas
Maine	Utah
Maryland	Virginia
Michigan	West Virginia
Minnesota	Wyoming

Source: Kenneth J. King, "Waiving Childhood Goodbye: How Juvenile Courts Fail to Protect Children from Unknowingly, Unintelligent and Involuntary Waivers of Miranda Rights," *Wisconsin Law Review* (2006): 431.

WHY WOULD A CHILD EVER ADMIT TO SOMETHING THAT SHE DIDN'T DO?

You may wonder why anyone, even a young child, would confess to a crime if she didn't do it. If a child is read a statement about her "right to remain silent," why would the child continue to give a statement?

Steven A. Drizin and Richard A. Leo have documented forty proven false juvenile confessions, including five from the infamous Central Park Jogger case.[2] There are many reasons, including the following, why children are more vulnerable when asked

TABLE 2.2 Police Questioning: States at a Glance

	Interested adult must be present during the interrogation if child is under a certain age		Child must have the opportunity to consult with an adult prior to the interrogation		The interrogation must be taped	
	YES	NO	YES	NO	YES	NO
Alabama		X		X		X
Alaska		X		X		X
Arizona		X		X		X
Arkansas		X		X		X
California		X		X		X
Colorado	X			X		X
Connecticut	X					
Delaware		X		X		X
Florida		X		X		X
Georgia		X		X		X
Hawaii		X		X		X
Idaho		X		X		X
Illinois		X		X		X
Indiana	X			X		X
Iowa		X	X			X
Kansas		X	X			X
Kentucky		X		X		X
Louisiana		X		X		X
Maine		X		X		X
Maryland		X		X		X
Massachusetts		X	X			X
Michigan		X		X		X

TABLE 2.2 Police Questioning . . . (*Continued*)

	Interested adult must be present during the interrogation if child is under a certain age		Child must have the opportunity to consult with an adult prior to the interrogation		The interrogation must be taped	
	YES	NO	YES	NO	YES	NO
Minnesota		X		X		X
Mississippi		X		X		X
Missouri		X		X		X
Montana		X	X			X
Nebraska		X		X		X
Nevada		X		X		X
New Hampshire		X		X		X
New Jersey		X	X			X
New Mexico		X	X			X
New York		X		X		X
North Carolina	X			X		X
North Dakota	X			X		X
Ohio		X		X		X
Oklahoma	X			X		X
Oregon		X		X		X
Pennsylvania		X		X		X
Rhode Island		X		X		X
South Carolina		X		X		X
South Dakota		X		X		X
Tennessee		X		X		X
Texas		X		X		X

(*Continued*)

TABLE 2.2 Police Questioning . . . (*Continued*)

	Interested adult must be present during the interrogation if child is under a certain age		Child must have the opportunity to consult with an adult prior to the interrogation		The interrogation must be taped	
	YES	NO	YES	NO	YES	NO
Utah		X		X		X
Vermont	X			X		X
Virginia		X		X		X
Washington		X	X			X
West Virginia		X		X		X
Wisconsin		X		X	X	
Wyoming		X		X		X

Source: Kenneth J. King, "Waiving Childhood Goodbye: How Juvenile Courts Fail to Protect Children from Unknowingly, Unintelligent and Involuntary Waivers of Miranda Rights," *Wisconsin Law Review* (2006): 431.

by a police officer to give a statement. This vulnerability may lead them to give false statements.

- Because their intellectual capacity is not fully developed, children are less likely to understand their Miranda rights.
- Additionally, minors are more likely to want to please and believe police officers because they are authority figures.
- Because juveniles are incapable of fully realizing the consequences of their decisions, they may confess because they believe it is the only way to end a psychologically coercive interrogation.[3]

WHAT IF MY CHILD HAS ALREADY GIVEN A STATEMENT?

If your child has given a statement, your attorney has the right to file a motion to suppress the statement. "Suppressing the statement" means that the prosecutor will not be able to use your child's statement as evidence in court. The statement can only be suppressed if there is evidence that it was coerced, or not voluntarily given. In making this decision, the judge will look at the "totality of the circumstances." Under the totality of the circumstances, judges look at many factors in deciding whether or not the statement was voluntary. Courts will first look at the child's personal characteristics, such as:

- How old was the child?
- What is his education and intelligence?
- Prior experience with law enforcement, including whether he has ever been arrested before.

The personal characteristics are balanced against the circumstances of the interrogation. For example:

- The length of the questioning
- The conditions under which the statements took place
- Any excessive physical or psychological pressure brought to bear on the child
- Any threats or methods used to compel a response
- Whether she was told she had the right to counsel and the right not to give a statement

"Pretrial motions" and whether your child's lawyer should consider filing one are discussed in chapter 5.

NOTES

1. *In re Jerrell* C.J. 283 Wis.2d 145 (2005).
2. Richard A. Leo and Steven A. Drizin, "The Problem of False Confessions in the Post DNA World," *North Carolina Law Review* 82 (2004): 891, 994.
3. See Jennifer J. Walters, "Comment, Illinois' Weakened Attempt to Prevent False Confessions by Juveniles: The Requirement of Counsel for the Interrogations of Some Juveniles," *Loyola University of Chicago Law Journal* 33 (2002): 487, 504–505. Cited in the *Jerrell* case.

3

Arrest

It is truly a scary thing to see a child you care about handcuffed and placed into a police car. For adults, the lack of control and lack of understanding about what will happen to the child while he is in custody adds anxiety to an already stressful situation. Once a child is in police custody, concerned adults may not have access to him until after the processing is complete. If you understand the process in advance you will be in the best position to protect him.

WHAT SHOULD I DO IF THE CHILD IS ALREADY IN POLICE CUSTODY?

When parents or guardians get a call that their child is in police custody, they should do the following:

1. Go down to the police station and ask to see the child. If you are permitted to see the child, instruct her not to give a statement. In addition, it is important to instruct the child

not to talk to cellmates, other people in custody, or visitors about the details of the case. Any statements she makes could be used against her.

Once I was representing a child named Randy. Randy's mother was brilliant. When I met her, she told me that when I went back in the cell room to see her son, I should use the word "fish." She had prepared for the day when her child might be separated from her and devised a family code word to be used so the child knew it was okay to talk. She told me that if I used the code word "fish," Randy would know that his mother thought he should talk to me.

2. Contact a lawyer. Whether or not you are permitted to see the child (and most likely you won't be until the processing is finished), try to contact a lawyer. If possible, the lawyer should go to the police station, inform the police that the child does not wish to give a statement, and ask to see the child. If the lawyer can't physically get to the station she should call. Again, the lawyer should instruct the police officer that the child is represented and is not to be questioned without an attorney present.

If you do not know a lawyer, contact the local public defender's office if there is one. In addition, you should also contact anyone you know who might know a lawyer who could help. This is the time to access your religious community and your neighbors. If you cannot see the child and cannot find a lawyer, wait in the station.

3. Take names. Regardless of whether you are able to see the child or not, write down the name and badge number of every officer you talk to, in addition to the name and badge number of the commanding officer.

WHAT WILL HAPPEN DURING ARREST PROCESSING?

The first thing that will happen to a child after being arrested is called "processing." Processing basically means that the police (and/or the prosecutor) will fill out paperwork and decide what to do with the case. In addition to paperwork, the following things are likely to take place.

- Mug shots and fingerprints. Part of the "processing" consists of having fingerprints and photos taken. States have different rules for how this information will be filed and made available.

- Charging. The police may work with the prosecutor to decide what crime the child will be charged with. At this point the child could be charged with anything from a summary offense (think traffic ticket) to a crime that could automatically send him to adult court (think murder), or anything in between. Charging decisions are within the police and or prosecutor's discretion. You will not have input into this decision.

- Intake process. During the intake process the juvenile probation department may gather information about the incident, the family, school attendance, and the child's living situation. A decision will also be made about whether the case is eligible for "diversion." Diversion means that the case is not serious enough to be sent on to the juvenile court. Diversion is a very good thing.

WHAT SHOULD I DO IF THE CHILD IS "WANTED" BY THE POLICE?

Confirm that there is actually is a warrant, not just talk of a warrant. There are two kinds of wanted. The first kind of "wanted" means that the police have "a suspicion" that your child was involved in some criminal act (or they have information about a criminal act) and they may get a warrant for your child. The second kind of "wanted" means that the police already have a warrant for the child's arrest.

If There Is No Warrant Yet

If the police do not have a warrant but are just talking about getting a warrant, the best thing to do is wait. Wait before you have your child talk to the police. Wait before your child turns himself in. In this situation, you have time, and you should use it to get good legal advice. If you have the luxury of time, consult with a lawyer and fill out a nonwaiver of rights form (see figure 2.1 for a sample). This is a piece of paper a child can carry around in his pocket in case he does get arrested. The nonwaiver of rights form explains to the police that the child has consulted with a lawyer and that he chooses not to give a statement.

If There Is a Warrant

If you have just been informed that a warrant exists for the arrest of your child, the best choice is to turn your child in. A warrant means the police have the legal right to arrest your child. Later, at pretrial, if you believe the warrant was defective for some reason, you can challenge it. But at this point, if a warrant has been signed, it's best to turn your child in for the following reasons:

- If the child turns herself in it will increase the chances of getting released after the arrest. In general, turning yourself in demonstrates to the state that you are not a flight risk and that you are a responsible person who will be cooperative with the judicial process.
- By turning herself in she will decrease the embarrassment of being hauled out of home or school unexpectedly.
- If your child turns herself in with a lawyer, or after consultation with a lawyer, it is less likely that a statement will be taken.

How and when you turn your child in is important. Again, try to prevent a statement being taken. In this case, you have a little more time and control, so you are better able to protect your child. Before you turn your child in you should call a lawyer or local public defender's office and get a nonwaiver of rights form signed.

OTHER PRACTICAL CONCERNS

The following are other practical concerns you can deal with before the child turns herself in:

- If possible, try to have a lawyer available by telephone or willing to come to the police station in case anything comes up.

For example, if it's been eight hours and the child is still being processed, it is helpful to have an attorney call. Or, if the decision is made to prosecute the child as an adult, the child will then have a bail hearing, and an attorney will be helpful.

- Dress the child in multiple layers of clothes, even if it is the middle of summer. You never know how hot or cold the holding cells will be, so my advice is always to dress for all situations. Dress in comfortable clothes, because it is likely to be a long wait.
- Make sure your child is well fed before she turns herself in. While juveniles do get fed while they are being processed, you never know exactly when or how much, so make sure something is in their stomachs before they go.
- Don't put things in their pockets—everything will be taken.

How Long Will My Child Be in Police Custody?
The Six-Hour Rule

Federal law prohibits keeping children in the police station for processing for more than six hours. The six-hour "clock" starts the moment a juvenile is placed in a secure custody situation, and it cannot be "turned off" until the child is removed from secure custody. For example, if a child is arrested and put in a police car at noon, the child should be out of the police station by six o'clock that night. This doesn't mean the child will be free to come home at six. If the case is serious, after processing, the child may be taken from the police station to the local juvenile detention center and held until the detention hearing. This rule just means that children can not stay in police station, sheriff's department, or jail for more than six hours.

If the child has been in police custody for more than six hours, do any or all of the following:

- Talk to the officer on duty.
- Take down her name and badge number.
- Ask to speak to her supervisor.
- Take down the supervisor's name and badge number.

- Calmly make all personnel aware of the six-hour rule.
- Continue to try and contact a lawyer.
- Stay in the station house until this issue is resolved.
- Discuss future remedies with the child's lawyer after the child is out of the police station.

Will My Child Be with Adult Prisoners?

No. First, you should be aware that whenever children are arrested, laws exist to keep them separate from adults. Under the Juvenile Justice and Delinquency Prevention Act, children must be "sight and sound" separated from adult prisoners. This means that children should not be able to see or hear them.

WHAT IF I *WANT* MY CHILD ARRESTED?

I've spoken with many parents who are beyond frustration and at a complete loss over what to do with their child. Some parents want to have their child arrested because they believe the child will have access to better mental health services. Some parents call because they think their child will get a better education in the justice system than the public schools. Some parents call because their child is involved in really dangerous activities, like running away, hanging out with gangs, or using drugs, and the parents are afraid the child will end up dead.

There are times when a parent has to call the police. For example, when parents are afraid that the child will harm them, they *should* call the police. More often, though, I see cases that are really a mother/daughter conflict, or a brother/sister fight, and I believe there are better ways for families to deal with these situations then getting juvenile court involved.

For parents thinking about calling the police to get their child arrested, remember this: once you make the call, you lose control. Once the arrest is made, you can't easily change your mind. It's not *your* case; it's the prosecution's case. Only the prosecutor can dismiss the charges, even if you later decide you don't want to proceed. You can't decide on Saturday night that you've had enough of your daughter's rude mouth, have her arrested, and then work it out on Tuesday and expect juvenile court to return her to your custody. Once your daughter is in the system there is a process, and many professionals will be evaluating what is going on with your daughter and in your home.

Some parents call the police because their son took their car without permission, only to decide later that he has "learned his lesson" and no longer needs to be in juvenile court. Parents, you need to look at this from a judge's perspective. Whenever parents call the police because of an out-of-control child, it generally means that they can't properly supervise the child and keep him safe. If that is true, and the court believes it, then how can a court quickly put the child back in their house and believe everything is going to be okay? If the problems were big enough for parents to want to get law enforcement involved, it is unlikely they can be resolved in a few days. Before the State dismisses the charges or the judge agrees to discharge a case, there will need to be evidence that something has changed. Has the child changed, or the parents? Has more supervision been put in place, has a mentor been arranged, or is Joey going to live with his uncle for a while?

Again, once you make the call, you lose control. The judge will now be making decisions for the child.

4

The Detention Hearing
Will They Keep the Child in Custody until Trial?

TOP TIPS

1. Show up. Attention all guardians, foster parents, and residential placement providers: it is critical that the child have someone present at the hearing who is willing to provide him with a place to live until trial. If the child is in a placement, determine whether or not the placement will allow the child to return.
2. Control yourself. Even if you completely disagree with the charges, this is not the time to argue with the court about it.
3. This is not the trial. The only purpose of this hearing is to decide where the child will live until the trial.
4. Bring good school reports or other indicators that the child is not a risk of flight or a danger to the community.
5. Attention school officials: if the event happened in school, was the child suspended or expelled? Be prepared to address whether or not the school is willing to allow the child to return.

Meet Thomas and Melissa. They had detention hearings the same week. Although Melissa was charged with having one marijuana cigarette in her pocket and Thomas was charged with rape, it was Melissa who was held in the detention center.

When the judge looked at Melissa's case, he saw the following situation: a fifteen-year-old girl who had a prior arrest and had missed her court date. He saw a school record with ninety unex-cused absences. There was a probation officer's report that said Melissa refused to cooperate and that she continued to test posi-tive for drugs, stay out late, and hang out with older men. Melissa's mother was in court and wanted to take her home; however, the mother had no explanation as to why Melissa missed her court date and why she was missing so much school. Despite the minor charges, Melissa was held in the detention center.

When the judge looked at Thomas's case, he noticed that this was a sixteen-year-old with his first arrest. Thomas was an honor student in the eleventh grade at a local high school and had perfect attendance. Both of his parents appeared on his behalf and assured the judge that they would cooperate fully with the court. The parents also offered to have Thomas live with rela-tives in order to be in a different school district from the victim. Thomas was released on electronic monitoring over the prose-cutor's objection.

It may be hard to make sense out of the cases of Thomas and Melissa, yet they demonstrate the unpredictable nature of deten-tion hearings. There are multiple factors a judge can consider when making detention decisions.

WHAT WILL HAPPEN AT THE DETENTION HEARING?

Imagine a laundry basket. At this stage the court is collecting information from a variety of sources and putting it all in the basket to be sorted out later. Information can come from any of the following places: the police, the victim, the prosecutor, the probation officer, the parents, and the school. This first hearing is sometimes called a "detention hearing," but sometimes it is called a "probable cause" or "pretrial hearing."

At the detention hearing the court will do three things:

1. Decide whether to hold the child in custody until the trial.
2. Determine whether there was probable cause for the arrest (which there almost always is).[1]
3. Handle administrative details such as passing discovery and setting a trial date.

DETENTION DECISIONS: HOW WILL THE JUDGE
DECIDE WHETHER OR NOT TO DETAIN MY CHILD?
WHAT CAN A CONCERNED ADULT DO?

To make a detention decision, a judge looks at many factors. However, there are only two purposes of detention:

1. To make sure the child comes back to court (is the child a flight risk?).
2. To make sure the child is not a danger to himself or the community.

If the judge believes that the child is a "flight risk" or that the child is "dangerous," the child will be held in detention until the next hearing.

Flight Risk: Can the Court Trust You to Get
This Child Back to Court?

In order to get a child released into an adult's custody until the next court date, the judge has to be convinced that the child is going to come back. Put yourself in the position of the judge. Judges don't want to look stupid. They want to look good to the other judges. So, when they decide to release a child, they want to be sure that someone is going to make sure the child comes back to court. This is kind of like a job interview for the concerned adult. Why should the court "hire you" for the job of shepherding the child through the system and making sure she gets to the next court date?

Is the Child a Danger to the Community (or Himself)?

The second question the court must ask before a child is released is whether the child presents a danger. A child can be a danger to the community if he is engaging in some kind of violent behavior. The court will look at what the current charges are against the child. Crimes considered violent or dangerous include assaults or fights, guns or other weapons, robbery, and rape or other sexual assaults. The court will also look at whether there are any prior arrests for aggressive or violent acts (such as probation/school). Is there a pattern of violence?

In addition to engaging in violent behavior, if there is information that the child may be a danger to herself, a court may consider detention. Behavior such as cutting, overdoses, and threats of self-violence will be considered. For example, if a few days before the arrest on a drug possession charge a girl took twenty Xanax pills in a suicide attempt, she could be considered a danger to herself.

In instances of violent behavior and self-injurious behavior, an adult can attempt to address the court's concerns by providing alternatives. For example, if a child keeps fighting, the guardian may come to court with anger management counseling already lined up. If the girl is threatening to harm herself, the guardian could arrange for counseling or a trauma screening. The more seriously the adult takes the concerns of the court, the more likely it is that the court will trust the adult to supervise the child until the next court date. It is not helpful to minimize the child's behavior by blaming the victim, the police, the school, or the situation. Even if you believe the child is only partially at fault, it is important to take responsibility for the situation and respectfully address the court's concerns.

THE TOP THREE FACTORS A JUDGE WILL LOOK AT IN DECIDING WHETHER TO DETAIN A CHILD

In my experience, when judges decide whether or not to release the child, they look at three main factors:

1. Is There a Stable, Concerned Adult Willing to Take the Child Home?

Above all else, a solid adult who appears on behalf of the child can make the difference in detention. An adult who appears concerned about the child, appropriately respectful of the situation, and understands the seriousness of juvenile court proceedings can help the judge feel secure in the fact that if the child is released, he will be returned to court. Everyone knows that kids are kids. It is unlikely that a child will be able to get to meetings with the lawyer and the probation officer or get himself to court-ordered evaluations on time. Judges know that the juvenile court process runs more smoothly when the child has an organized responsible adult.

What if the child's parent is not available? While a parent is preferable, the concerned adult does not have to be a parent. In most jurisdictions, guardians, placement providers, foster parents, and extended family members such as aunts and uncles who appear on the child's behalf and appear responsible, are all fine.

When evaluating flight risk, judges look to see if the adult has ties to the community. The more tied to the community, the less likely the family or child will leave the jurisdiction. When looking at ties to the community, some combination of the following is helpful:

- Has a work history
- Has lived in the neighborhood or city for a length of time (preferably for several years)
- Is involved in a religious community
- Owns a home

2. School Record

For many judges, a child's school record is a major factor in deciding whether to release a child. The school record is used as a window into the child's world and can tell the court what kind of supervision the child was receiving at home prior to the arrest.

What if my child has a poor school report? Let's say a child shows up and the school record reveals all Fs, or that he has missed a lot of days (and anything over twenty is a lot of days), or that he has already been suspended three times this year for fights. In all of these situations, the judge will get the impression that the child does not have enough supervision or support in the house. As the adult, it is important to acknowledge your role in the situation and what you will do in the future to address the issues.

What if my child has attendance issues and failing grades? This is a major problem and as a concerned adult, you need to address why this is happening and what you are going to do differently in the future. A judge will likely assume that truancy and failing grades are a result of the following:

- Lack of parental control. For example, maybe the parent gets the child up every day and puts her on the bus, but then the child never actually gets to school. Instead the child decides to hang out at the local store. Or the child goes to school but just hangs out with her friends in the parking lot or the cafeteria. Even if this is not the parent's fault, the question becomes, "Are the parents aware of the situation, and what actions are they taking to address it?"
- Instability in the house. The missed days may be attributed to the overwhelming problems of the parent. For example, maybe the health concerns of the parent/sibling/grandparent prevent the child from going to school because he needs to stay home and take care of a family member. Or maybe a recent move or divorce has disrupted school attendance.
- Undiagnosed/unaddressed learning disability. Attendance problems are frequently a result of an undiagnosed learning disability that causes the child embarrassment every day, and to avoid the embarrassment, the child cuts school. (See chapter 14, "Special Education Issues," for more detail.)
- Bullying/gang issues. If children are afraid of being recruited into a gang, or are being bullied, they may choose to avoid the situation by failing to come to school.

If the child's school record is a disaster, release is still possible, but a concerned adult needs to appear and be willing to take responsibility for the situation. Take responsibility by acknowledging the problem and your role in it. Offer a plausible explanation for why it occurred, if appropriate, and tell the court what you will do in the future to make sure the child's educational needs are addressed.

What if my child has a good school report? A good school report sends a very positive message to the judge. When the school record is good, it implies the following:

- The family values education.
- The child has the appropriate support to get there on time with the necessary school supplies.
- The home environment is a place where schoolwork can get done.

Grades don't have to be perfect. Grades of Bs and Cs are okay, even an occasional D/F, but the child needs to be in school to give a judge confidence that an adult can get the child back to court. *Note:* If the school record is good, bring it to court with you.

3. Has the Child Missed Court Before?

Finally, in deciding if the child is a flight risk, the court will look to see if there have been any other times the child missed court. If the child missed a court date before, you will need to address it with an explanation of why it happened and what you will do differently this time to make sure it doesn't happen again.

Once the court date was missed, did the child turn herself in soon after the missed date? Or did she stay out on the street for several months or several years? Obviously, the longer the time between the missed court date and turning himself in, the less likely it is that the court will release the child.

CAN MY CHILD GET BAIL?

Under the U.S. Constitution and many state constitutions, children do not have a right to bail. However, some states have made provisions for children (really, their families) to post bail for release. See table 4.1.

TABLE 4.1 Can the Child Get Bail?

STATES THAT DO NOT ALLOW BAIL FOR JUVENILES		
Alabama	Maine	Oregon
Alaska	Maryland	Pennsylvania
Arizona	Minnesota	Rhode Island
California	Mississippi	South Carolina
District of Columbia	Missouri	South Dakota
Florida	New Hampshire	Tennessee
Hawaii	New Jersey	Texas
Idaho	New Mexico	Utah
Illinois	New York	Vermont
Indiana	North Carolina	Virginia
Iowa	North Dakota	Wisconsin
Kentucky	Ohio	Wyoming
	Oklahoma	

STATES THAT ALLOW BAIL FOR JUVENILES	
Arkansas (bond)	Michigan
Colorado	Missouri
Connecticut	Montana
Delaware	Nebraska
Georgia	Nevada
Kansas (bond)	Washington (bond)
Louisiana	West Virginia
Massachusetts	

Source: National Juvenile Defender Center, "Legal Strategies to Reduce the Unnecessary Detention of Children," *Advocacy and Training Guide* (Fall 2004): 159.

WHAT ELSE WILL HAPPEN AT THE DETENTION HEARING? ADMINISTRATIVE DETAILS
Discovery May Be Received

Discovery is the police paperwork about the arrest and it may be given to the child or the child's attorney at this stage. The discovery will include a summary of the facts of the case, the charges against the child, and statements from any witnesses.

A Lawyer May Be Appointed

If the child cannot afford to hire a lawyer, the court should appoint one at the earliest possible date. The court may ask the family of the child to fill out information to see if its income level qualifies for an appointed counsel or public defender. (I am not aware of any courts where proof or tax returns are needed.) Different jurisdictions have different income levels. However, if a lawyer is not appointed and you feel you cannot afford one, there are other options. The family may request that the judge reconsider the appointment of counsel, or the local bar association may be a resource. In some jurisdictions, law school clinical programs may be resources. (See the resource list at the end of this book.)

A Trial Date, or Next Court Date, May Be Set

If the child is held in custody, there should be a quicker court date than if the child was released. In some states, when a child is in custody, a trial must occur within ten days; in others it is thirty days. Since most jurisdictions try to avoid the overcrowding of youth detention centers, it is in everyone's interest to set quick trial dates to minimize the time children spend in detention.

Evaluations May Be Ordered

The court may order evaluations to better understand the child's needs. For example, if the child has mental health issues, the court can order a psychological exam. See chapter 16, "Children with Mental Health Issues," for more information about mental health evaluations.

The Prosecutor May Convey Offer to Resolve the Case

Even at this early stage, the prosecutor may decide to convey an offer to resolve the case. *Do not feel rushed to take an offer if you don't really understand the consequences.* Most probably you have not had an opportunity to discuss the case fully with a lawyer, and even if you did have, the lawyer was just handed discovery. There will always be another opportunity for the child to admit guilt.

Take your time. However, there is one offer that should be given serious consideration even at this early stage. That is the offer to "divert" the case. See the more detailed discussion of diversion in Frequently Asked Question 5 at the end of this chapter.

CAUTION: WHAT *NOT* TO DO AT THE DETENTION HEARING

First, remember that the detention hearing is not a trial. Even if you think the police were completely wrong to arrest the child, this is not the time to argue about it. Don't take your frustration about the situation out on the judge or anyone else in the courtroom. Remember, a big factor in whether the child gets released is whether or not the adult who shows up in court appears responsible and appreciates the seriousness of the situation. As an adult, whether you agree with the facts or not, you must respect the judicial system. Making a lot of excuses for your child and refusing to take any responsibility for the situation will diminish the judge's opinion of your ability to parent.

Second, be aware that detention hearings are usually tape recorded. Even if the hearing is not tape recorded, there are prosecutors and other law enforcement officers all around you and everything you say can be used against you later.

Let's say, for example, that your daughter was arrested for a fight with another girl over some boy. During the course of the fight, your daughter pulls a razor out of her bra and cuts the other girl on the arm. Now, you know that there is more to the incident than just the razor cut. You know that the other girl had a bat and that your daughter was trying to defend herself. At the detention hearing everyone is focused on how bad your daughter is— issuing restraining orders, talking about detention. What should you do? Stay quiet and be respectful to the court. Save everything you want to say for a future conversation with your lawyer. Your *only* objective at this hearing is to get your daughter released from custody. If you are disrespectful to the other girl's mother when you see her in court, it will count as a strike against you. The court is looking for adults who can be positive role models for children. Calling the other girl's mother names or threatening retaliation is the surest way to hurt your interests.

Finally, appearances count. Dress conservatively. This means ditch the midriff shirt, the eyebrow, nose, and navel piercing, and cover all tattoos. Dress as if you are going to a religious service. T-shirts with "funny slogans" are not funny in court. If the concerned adult is wearing a shirt that says "You know you want me," it will be perceived as disrespectful to the court.

FREQUENTLY ASKED QUESTIONS

1. My Child Has Been Out of Control. If I Agree to Let Him Come Home, How Do I Know Things Will Be Different?

This is an extremely common concern. Adults want to do the right thing; they don't want to abandon their child, yet they know that up to this point there have been a lot of problems. For example, maybe the child has been disrespectful and defiant at home. Or many the parents are genuinely worried about their child's safety and are concerned he will be killed out on the streets.

Most jurisdictions have many pretrial detention options; it is usually not just a choice between the detention facility and going home. If a concerned adult wants to take the child home, support is usually available from the court to help him control his child. The following is a list of options that may be available:

- In-home detention. The court orders very strict conditions on the child's home life, such as reporting to a probation officer or a mentor who checks in with the child every day after school.
- Electronic monitoring program. This is an ankle bracelet that constantly monitors the child's location. This is the most restrictive option that still keeps the child at home. It can be very effective. However, the bracelet can be seen, especially in the summer months, and could cause some embarrassment to the child.
- Alternative living arrangement. In some situations, when the victim lives near the child who was arrested, the court will want to make sure that there is no contact. Sometimes the best thing to do is have the child who was arrested live

somewhere else until the trial is over. While this can be very disruptive to school and other activities, it is certainly preferable to detention.

2. I Think Some Tough Love Will Teach Her a Lesson.
Won't a Little Time in Detention Be Good for Her?

There was a father in Pittsburgh who wanted to scare his kid straight and dropped him off at a detention center where his buddy worked the night shift. While there, the child got a broken arm. The detention center was sued.

There are times when adults feel so out of control that detention becomes a very attractive option. Be aware, though, that there are many dangers to holding children in detention.

First, remember that a detention center is only to hold children until the trial. Detention centers are not treatment centers. If your child has mental health issues, a detention center is not a psychiatric facility, and the staff may not be trained to monitor your child's behavior. For a child with mental health issues, being in detention could make things worse by adding a lot of stress.

Second, studies have repeatedly shown that detention has a negative impact on children. Children placed in detention are more likely to receive harsher penalties after trial and more likely to engage in further criminal activity. Think about it. By placing a child in detention you are putting her in the company of the worst possible peer group. What will she learn while she is there?

Third, there are particular dangers if the detention centers are overcrowded. When facilities are crowded they become unsafe for the staff and the children.

3. The Judge Has Decided to Detain My Child.
What Should I Do Now?

- Inform the detention center and your child's lawyer about any medications the child is taking. Make sure that the medication is dropped off at the detention center.
- Work with the child's lawyer to develop the best trial strategy and disposition plan.

- Visit the child frequently. Find out the visiting hours in advance and be sure to ask about any regulations. Are younger siblings allowed to visit? What kind of ID is needed? Can you bring your child things from home, such as books, magazines, or money for the purchase of sundries?

4. Should My Child Admit the Charges at the Detention Hearing?

The answer to this is: only if the prosecutor is offering diversion.

Generally, I advise adults to *wait* before encouraging their child to admit to any charges. I believe it is necessary to have time to thoroughly review the evidence and consider the consequences. There is one exception, however, and that is when the prosecutor is offering to divert the case.

5. What Does "Diversion" Mean?

There are many kinds of diversion, but if the prosecutor offers a diversionary program where the child does *not* have to admit guilt, and there is a guarantee that if the child does well the case will be erased from the child's record, that is an offer to consider seriously. (Refer back to figure 1.1 to get a better understanding of why diversion is such a great deal.) Diversion programs take the child's case out of the juvenile justice system and avoid all the risk and potential long-term consequences of juvenile court involvement.

Seriously consider diversion programs that have the following components:

- No admission of guilt
- Period of probation/community service
- No long-term juvenile record (guaranteed expungement)

What if my child is innocent? Won't taking the diversionary program make him look guilty? No. There is no admission of guilt. This is a hard concept for most adults to get, but this is a safe way out of the system with no long-term record. The reason I would advise my own brother to take a diversion deal is this: although

TABLE 4.2 Detention Hearing Issues: States at a Glance

After the arrest, how long will the child wait for a detention hearing?		Will a lawyer be appointed at the hearing?
Alabama	Within 72 hours of detention, weekends and holidays included.	Yes
Alaska	Within 48 hours of notice to the court of detention.	Yes
Arizona	Within 24 hours of filing petition.	Yes
Arkansas	Within 72 hours of custody. If falls on weekend or holiday, then next business day.	Unlikely
California	As soon as possible, but at least before the expiration of the next day after the petition is filed.	Maybe
Colorado	Within 48 hours of detention, excluding weekends and legal holidays.	Maybe
Connecticut	Next business day following arrest.	Unlikely
Delaware	Peace officer takes youth, "without reasonable delay" to Family Court for detention hearing or to another court until Family Court's next session.	Unlikely
District of Columbia	No later than the next day (excluding Sundays) after taken into custody.	Yes
Florida	Within 24 hours of custody unless for failure to appear, then 72 hours.	Yes
Georgia	Within 72 hours after placed in detention unless deadline falls on Saturday, Sunday, or holiday, in which case, next business day.	Unlikely
Hawaii	Child shall be taken without unnecessary delay to court, no precise deadline.	Maybe
Idaho	Within 24 hours of preliminary decision to release or detain following apprehension, excluding weekends and holidays.	Maybe
Illinois	Within 40 hours of detention, excluding weekends and holidays.	Yes
Indiana	No later than 48 hours of excluding weekends and holidays.	Yes

TABLE 4.2 Detention Hearing Issues . . . (*Continued*)

After the arrest, how long will the child wait for a detention hearing?		Will a lawyer be appointed at the hearing?
Iowa	Within 24 hours of detention, excluding weekends and holidays.	Yes
Kansas	Within 48 hours of detention, excluding weekends and holidays.	Yes
Kentucky	Within 48 hours of detention, excluding weekends and holidays; within 24 hours of detention, excluding weekends and holidays if status offender.	Unlikely
Louisiana	Judge reviews police statement on probable cause within 48 hours of custody. If child is not released, continued custody hearing within 3 days of entry into detention center.	Maybe
Maine	Within 48 hours of detention, excluding weekends and holidays.	Unlikely
Maryland	No later than next day after petition filed (petition must be filed immediately upon detention).	Unlikely
Massachusetts	Within the next day of entering any detention facility.	Maybe
Michigan	Within 24 hours of being taken into custody, excluding Sundays and holidays.	Maybe
Minnesota	Within 36 hours, excluding weekends and holidays; within 24 hours, excluding weekends and holidays, if held in an adult facility.	Yes
Mississippi	Within 48 hours of detention, excluding weekends and state holidays.	Maybe
Missouri	Within 3 days of detention, excluding weekends and holidays.	Maybe
Montana	Within 24 hours of being taken into custody, excluding weekends and legal holidays.	Maybe
Nebraska	Within 24 hours of custody, excluding days court is not in session.	Maybe

(*Continued*)

TABLE 4.2 Detention Hearing Issues . . . (*Continued*)

After the arrest, how long will the child wait for a detention hearing?		Will a lawyer be appointed at the hearing?
Nevada	Within 72 hours of detention, excluding weekends and holidays; within 24 hours if the juvenile submits a written application for hearing.	Maybe
New Hampshire	Within 24 hours of being taken into custody, excluding Sundays and holidays.	Yes
New Jersey	No later than the morning after placement in detention, including weekends and holidays.	Unlikely
New Mexico	Within 24 hours of filing petition, excluding weekends and holidays. The petition must be filed within 24 hours of custody.	Maybe
New York	Within 72 hours of whichever comes first: detention or next day court is in session.	Yes
North Carolina	Within 5 calendar days if held in secure custody; 7 calendar days if non-secure.	Yes
North Dakota	Promptly, and no later than 96 hours after detention.	Maybe
Ohio	Promptly, but no later than 72 hours after detention.	Maybe
Oklahoma	Next day after custody, or by 2 judicial days if good cause is shown.	Unlikely
Oregon	Within 36 hours, excluding weekends and judicial holidays, except on order of the court.	Unlikely
Pennsylvania	Within 72 hours of detention.	Maybe
Puerto Rico	Probable cause hearing to be held within 7 days of apprehension, or "without unnecessary delay" if apprehended under court order.	Unlikely
Rhode Island	A child shall be referred to the Family Court within 24 hours of detention.	Yes
South Carolina	Within 48 hours of custody, excluding weekends and holidays.	Yes

TABLE 4.2 Detention Hearing Issues . . . (*Continued*)

After the arrest, how long will the child wait for a detention hearing?		Will a lawyer be appointed at the hearing?
South Dakota	Within 48 hours of custody, excluding weekends and holidays.	Unlikely
Tennessee	Within 3 days of detention, excluding days court is not in session.	Maybe
Texas	No later than second business day after taken into custody. If juvenile is detained on Friday or Saturday, then no later than first working day.	Maybe
Utah	Within 48 hours of being taken into custody, excluding weekends and holidays, unless continuance has been granted.	Maybe
Vermont	Within 48 hours of initial court order of custody, excluding weekends and holidays.	Yes
Virginia	On next day in which court sits within city or county where child is taken into custody; if court does not sit on next day, no later than 72 hours.	Maybe
Washington	Probable cause determination within 48 hours of being taken into custody if no arrest warrant. Detention hearing within 72 hours of filing petition, which must be filed within 72 hours of placement into custody.	Unlikely
West Virginia	Without delay, and no later than the next day after custody.	No
Wisconsin	Within 24 hours after the end of the day on which the decision to detain was made, excluding Saturdays, Sundays, and legal holidays.	Yes
Wyoming	Within 72 hours of being taken into custody if juvenile is detained without court order.	Maybe

Source: National Juvenile Defender Center, "Legal Strategies to Reduce the Unnecessary Detention of Children," *Advocacy and Training Guide* (Fall 2004): 84.

you agree to be monitored for a period of time, it's the way to get a guarantee that the case will go away. In some jurisdictions, it is rare that a child will be found completely innocent of all charges. Many judges find children guilty of something, even if it is a lesser charge, because they believe they need "help."

NOTES

1. "Probable cause" is a legal term that refers to whether the police had a reason to arrest the child. Basically, the judge will find probable cause when there is reason to believe that a crime was committed and that the child committed the offense. Usually, since the child just got arrested, the judge is going to find probable cause. Again, this is not a trial, and a finding of probable cause does not mean your child will ultimately be found guilty.

    The procedure of the probable cause hearing differs from state to state. Sometimes the judicial determination of probable cause does not occur in court. A judge may read the police statements and make a determination based on that alone. Sometimes a first appearance in court is solely a probable cause determination. In these jurisdictions, the issue of whether detention is appropriate is considered at a later hearing. Since procedures differ so dramatically, working with a lawyer is essential.

5

Pretrial Issues
What to Do between the Detention Hearing and the Trial

TOP TIPS

1. If the judge allowed the child to live at home until the trial, make sure the child:
   - Abides by *all* of the judge's conditions including curfew
   - Goes to school every day
   - Stays away from the victim and the victim's family
2. If the judge held the child in detention, you should:
   - Visit the child
   - Make sure the detention center is aware of any medications the child may be taking
3. Regardless of where the child is living, gather information to give to the child's attorney about potential witnesses and important information about the child's background.

Sean was arrested for robbery. According to the police report he came up from behind the victim, pushed him to the ground, and took his iPod. At the detention hearing the judge allowed Sean to go back home on the condition that he be placed on electronic monitoring (a small metal ankle bracelet that could track exactly when he was out of the house). While on electronic monitoring Sean could only be at home or school: no after-school activities were allowed and no weekend activities except church. This was Sean's first arrest, and he insisted that he was innocent. He even had an alibi. There were several witnesses, including Megan's mom, who would come to court and say that

Sean couldn't have done this because he was at Megan's house that night.

After two weeks of being on electronic monitoring, Sean was extremely stressed. He felt the whole situation was completely unfair. In his anger, he told his mother that he was going to cut off the bracelet—an action that would certainly land him in the detention center and look bad for his case. Sean's mother worried constantly. She knew Sean was an emotional fifteen-year-old, and she worried that he might run away and end up with a bench warrant. The last thing Sean's mom wanted was more trouble with the police.

The pretrial stage of a juvenile court hearing can be extremely important. If the child does well (either at home or in detention) this sheds a positive light on the child. Success at home or on electronic monitoring shows the court that the child can be supervised at home. It shows that the child will take the judge's rules seriously and that the living situation is able to provide appropriate structure.

However, if during the pretrial phase a child continues to act out, this sheds a very negative light on the child. For example, if while home the child continues to stay out all night or refuse to go to school, this sends a message to the court that the child will not listen to authority and may not be able to handle being out in the community. If the child is on electronic monitoring and impulsively cuts off the ankle bracelet, that act can be seen as a deliberate disregard for the court, and confirm that the child is a flight risk and should be held in detention.

This stage of the process can be extremely difficult for concerned adults. Concerned adults may feel guilt, helplessness, and confusion about what to do. They may see the child's point of view and believe that the restrictions placed on the child are too severe. They may want to help the child and even enable the child to go beyond what the judge ordered. This is a huge mistake. The court is trusting the guardian and the child to be able to abide by court rules. Violation of that trust can result in very damaging future consequences and make the difference between a child getting probation or placement if found guilty.

The best advice is this: stay calm and encourage the child to stick to the rules. Remind the child that the restrictions are just for a little while, not forever. Just deal with it for today. Get other responsible adults that the child trusts to repeat this message. Do what the judge ordered. It matters.

In addition to helping the child abide by the court's rules, concerned adults should do the following in the pretrial stage:

- Stay away from the victim and the victim's family.
- Gather information that can help the child's case.

DON'T HAVE ANY CONTACT WITH
THE VICTIM OR THE VICTIM'S FAMILY

It is particularly important not to have any contact with the victim or the victim's family. If your case involves someone that the child knows, you should make every effort to avoid the victim until the trial is over. There is a fine line between trying to "talk to the victim about what happened" and harassment. It can be extremely damaging to the case and to the ultimate disposition if the judge perceives the child or parent as intimidating the witness or encouraging the witness not to come to court to make the case go away. If the court receives information that Dad is following the victim in the grocery store trying to get a statement, it will reflect negatively on the stability of the dad and impact the court's willingness to allow the child to remain at home.

GATHERING INFORMATION TO HELP THE CHILD'S CASE

First, let's talk about what concerned adults should *not* do.

Don't take the process into your own hands. It is *not* a good idea for the concerned adult to be the investigator. A vigilante mom can make things significantly worse for the child. As a concerned adult, you can be very helpful by providing potential witness information to the child's attorney, but you will harm the child's case if you start stalking neighbors.

What *can* a concerned adult do to assist in the investigation?

Concerned adults can be extremely valuable in the investigation of a child's case. In particular, concerned adults can do the following:

- Gather important information about the child. This includes school reports or medical reports that can be used at trial, in negotiation with the prosecutor, or at disposition
- Provide the names and contact information of witnesses who might be willing to testify on the child's behalf.

Gathering Witness Contact Information

There are a variety of witnesses that might be helpful to the child's case. I will focus on the three types of witnesses that are commonly used:

- Eyewitnesses
- Fact witnesses
- Character witnesses

Both eyewitnesses and fact witnesses can testify about the incident. Eyewitnesses are persons who were there and saw the incident. Fact witnesses are persons who can testify to a specific fact about the case. Character witnesses may not have any connection to the incident but can say that the child enjoys a good reputation in the community.

Eyewitnesses and fact witnesses. A good place to start in determining who might be an eyewitness or a fact witness is the police report. By reading the police report you will learn where and when the incident happened. Once you know the crime scene, you can determine who might have seen the incident.

For example, if the incident happened in the school cafeteria, there is a good chance that some of the other students who were eating lunch saw what happened. The child could give a list of student names to his attorney for the attorney to investigate.

Some eyewitnesses will not want to be involved. Again, all you can do is give the information to the child's attorney and let go. Your child's attorney and the court have the power to subpoena a witness to court, but that is not something for a concerned adult to take on.

Fact witnesses are those witnesses that may not have seen the incident, but can provide information about a piece of the case. For example, Robert is arrested for stealing $40 from Joey. The prosecutor is using the money found in Robert's pocket as evidence against him. A fact witness for Robert might be his Uncle Steve, who could testify that he gave Robert $50 for his birthday the day before the incident. Uncle Steve cannot say whether or not Robert stole the money, but he can give an explanation for why money was in Robert's pocket.

Good character witnesses. "Good character" is evidence that can be presented through witnesses to tell the court why the crime charged is completely out of character for this child. For example, if Matthew is arrested for having a fight and the victim gets sent to the hospital for a broken nose, the child's attorney could present a character witness to say that Matthew has a reputation for being nonviolent. A character witness for Matthew would say that fighting is uncharacteristic of Matthew. Or, for example, if a child is charged with stealing a car and joyriding, the attorney could present evidence that the child enjoys a reputation for being honest and truthful.

A concerned adult can be extremely helpful in locating potential character witnesses. Once you identify these witnesses, give the names and contact information to the child's lawyer.

The best character witnesses are people who:

- Know the child well,
- Are not members of the child's own family,
- Are upstanding members of the community themselves (that is, the witness has no criminal record of her own),
- Can be articulate witnesses in court.

The following is a list of individuals who could be good character witnesses:

- Sports coach
- Teacher
- Neighbor
- Religious figure
- Employer

A character witness does not testify that the child did not commit the crime. Rather, the character witness testifies that this child has a reputation for being law-abiding, truthful, and nonviolent. This testimony allows the judge to determine that, based on the reputation of his good character, it is unlikely that the child would do this.

Typical character testimony goes like this:

Child's attorney: "Mrs. Jones, do you know Johnny?"

Mrs. Jones: "Yes."

Child's attorney: "Can you describe how you know Johnny?"

Mrs. Jones: "I've been the pastor at the local church and I've known Johnny his whole life."

Child's attorney: "Do you know other people in the community who know Johnny?"

Mrs. Jones: "Yes, I do."

Child's attorney: "What kind of reputation does Johnny enjoy in the community?"

Mrs. Jones: "Johnny has an excellent reputation, and is always taking out the trash for the elderly."

Can my child still have good character if she has been arrested before? Character witnesses are generally most effective when there are no prior arrests. There are some occasions when character witnesses may be presented even if there have been prior arrests, but this is an issue to discuss with the child's attorney. Remember, even if the character witness can't be used during the trial, he might be extremely helpful at the disposition hearing. A room full of community support encourages the judge to allow the child to remain at home.

ROLE OF THE CHILD'S ATTORNEY
DURING THE PRETRIAL STAGE

Although this book is written for concerned adults, it is helpful to understand what the child's lawyer should be doing at this stage in the process. Understanding the legal terms of the pretrial process can help you work with the child's attorney. The following are three main areas of the attorney's pretrial responsibilities.

- Discovery. In the discovery process, the child's attorney is requesting as much information as possible from the prosecutor. By reviewing the police reports and witness statements, the child and his family are in a better position to see how the state will prove the case against the child.
- Investigation. During investigation the defense attorney is gathering information about the child's case.
- Pretrial motions. There are many kinds of pretrial motions, but one of the most important is the pretrial motion to suppress evidence. By filing a pretrial motion the child's attorney may be able to get rid of certain evidence if it was obtained in an unlawful way.

The Discovery Process: Reviewing the Police Paperwork
to Understand the Evidence against the Child

When an arrest is made, many reports are created. These reports are also known as "discovery." Reviewing these reports can help you understand what evidence the state has against the child. In general, when a child is arrested, there will be some type of statement from the arresting officer in addition to information about witnesses and any physical evidence that was found (like money or stolen property.)

The discovery process is like playing Go Fish. Here the child's attorney can request information from the prosecutor. Sometimes the prosecutor is obligated to turn it over. Sometimes the prosecutor is not. When the prosecutor refuses to turn the documents over, the child's attorney has the choice between forgoing the information or requesting it from the court. For example:

Child's attorney: "Please give me a copy of the police report."
Prosecutor: "Okay."
Child's attorney: "Please give me a copy the witness statements."
Prosecutor: "Okay."
Child's attorney: "Please give me a list of all the people who made prior complaints against this officer for brutality in the past five years."
Prosecutor: "Go Fish."

Discovery is a legal term that means information and/or evidence that the state has about the case. Under the discovery rules a person who has been arrested is entitled to know what evidence the state has against him before going to trial.

The two most important things to know about discovery are as follows:

1. The child's attorney must request discovery.
2. The child's attorney is entitled to evidence that will help your child's case.

The United States Supreme Court in the case of *Brady v. Maryland*, U.S. 83 (1963), held that it is the prosecutor's *duty* to provide any material and exculpatory evidence to defense counsel upon request. This means that if there is evidence that implies the child did not do the crime, the prosecutor has to give it to the child's attorney.

Although every state has different discovery rules, generally, a person who was charged with a crime will be entitled to the following:

- Police report
- Petition against the child

You *might* be entitled to the following:

- List of the state's witnesses
- Copies of witness statements
- Results from tests (drug tests for the contents of the drugs found, breath tests for alcohol consumption)
- Other evidence that is documentary or physical in nature (photos or videos that were taken, reports from state experts such as the fire marshal in an arson case)

Is There Any Information That the Child's Lawyer Has to Give the State?

Yes, discovery goes both ways. The child's attorney may have to provide discovery to the state. For example, many states give the prosecution the right to get the following information from the defense:

- Names (and sometimes statements) of witnesses the defense may call.
- Witness information, including address and other contact information. The prosecutor may actually talk to the witnesses listed or may just use the information to run a criminal records check. If one of your witnesses has a prior criminal record, this record could be used to "impeach" or test the credibility the witnesses.
- Reports from any defense experts that may be called.
- Tangible evidence that may have been recovered.
- Alibi notice. An alibi defense is one in which the child asserts that she could not have done the crime because she wasn't there. If a child asserts this defense, she will have to provide "alibi notice." Alibi notice is information about who will be called to testify that in fact the child was not in the location where the crime was committed at the time it was committed.

Frequently Asked Questions about Discovery

1. **What if my child tells the lawyer that she did it? Does the lawyer have to reveal that?** No. All discussions between the child who has been arrested and the attorney are confidential, so

discussions about the case and case strategy are not discoverable by the state. This protection is part of the Fifth Amendment right against self-incrimination. Let's say for example that during an interview with her attorney, the child admits that yes, she did break into the victim's car and steal all the property inside because she was so angry that her boyfriend dumped her. Is Lisa's attorney allowed to tell the prosecutor that in fact Lisa is guilty? No. The attorney for the child is bound by the rules of ethics not to disclose what her clients tell her unless the client (Lisa) gives permission.

2. What if we investigate someone as a witness and then don't want to use them? Do we have to give that information to the prosecutor? No. This is called "attorney work product" and you don't have to turn it over. Let's say for example that you talk to a potential witness named Melanie Jones. Melanie Jones tells you that she thinks the child should be locked up because he is always hanging around, causing trouble. Obviously you wouldn't want to call this witness. Under the rules of discovery, since you are not calling the witness you would not have to turn over information about her.

Pretrial Motions to Suppress: Getting Rid of Evidence That Can Hurt You

Imagine that a police officer pulls over a seventeen-year-old boy for running a red light. Should the officer be able to search the glove compartment or trunk of the car? What if the officer followed him home before he stopped him, could the officer search his garage?

Imagine that a police officer gets an anonymous tip that people are selling drugs on the corner of Eighth and York. Can the police go into the pockets of all the people standing on that corner?

Imagine that a middle school principal has heard rumors that students are bringing drugs to school. Can he do a random locker search of the entire seventh grade class?

The preceding examples illustrate the kind of issues that are involved in a pretrial motion to suppress. It is here that the defense has an opportunity to exclude evidence that is harmful to the child's case if the police gained the evidence unlawfully. As a concerned adult, it is important to understand the concept behind pretrial motions to suppress because it applies to a number of situations and can dramatically alter the strategy of defense. This section is designed to highlight the issues involved so that a concerned adult can intelligently discuss the issues with the child's attorney. There are numerous other pretrial motions that an attorney can make on behalf of a child, but this chapter will only briefly focus on pretrial motions to suppress.

What is a "pretrial motion to suppress" and why is it so important? A "pretrial motion" is a document the child's defense attorney can file with the court saying that there needs to be a hearing before the trial. This hearing is not about guilt or innocence.

"Motion to suppress" is a way for the child's attorney to say to the court that the state got the evidence unlawfully and should not be allowed to use it. The word "suppress" is another way to say "exclude."

Suppression arguments usually rely on the Fourth Amendment of the Constitution, which guarantees the right against "unreasonable search and seizure." The reason motions to suppress evidence are so important is because when certain evidence is excluded, the prosecutor may be unable to prove the case, which increases the likelihood that the child will be found not guilty.

What kind of evidence can be suppressed?

- Physical evidence. This includes money, drugs, stolen property, and any other physical evidence connecting the child to the crime.
- Identification evidence. If the identification procedure used by the police is "unnecessarily suggestive," it may be suppressed. For example, let's say the police handcuff your child and put him in the back of the police car and drive him to the location of the victim. The police then ask the victim if this is the person who did it. This kind of identification, where the victim sees the child already handcuffed and in police custody, may be suggestive and may be suppressible.
- Statements made by the child to the police (see chapter 2).

How do I know if my child's case has a good motion to suppress?

Step one. You need a search, personal standing, and government action.

First there must have been a "search or a seizure." For physical evidence that was found on or near your child, generally, every time a child gets arrested there is going to be a search and or seizure. A "seizure" happens when the child is arrested. There is usually a "search" of the child's person immediately after the arrest.

Next, you need "personal standing." The person who was searched has to assert that there was an unlawful search or seizure. A person can only make a claim under the Fourth Amendment on behalf of himself or herself, not a third party. A person must show that that his or her person, house, or car has been subjected to a governmental search. Each person has to assert their own rights.

Third, you need "government action." The search must have been conducted by a government official or by someone acting as an agent for the government. For example, a mom who decides to search her son's room for drugs or read her daughter's diary does not fall under the Fourth Amendment, no matter how unreasonable the search might be. A search by a police officer is obviously government action. However, the court has found that searches by the following types of people also count as government action:

- School officials
- Firefighters
- Public hospital employees
- Building inspectors
- Government employee supervisors

Step two. Was the search or seizure unreasonable?

After you make sure there is personal standing and government action, the next question is whether the search or seizure was unreasonable. The search of a person or private property or the seizure of a person or private property has to be unreasonable to be in violation of the Fourth Amendment. "Unreasonable" is one of those mushy legal words whose definition is hard to pin down. Generally, the court tries to balance the privacy interests of the person against the government's interest in doing the search or seizure.

The courts decide whether the search or seizure is unreasonable by looking at the "totality of the circumstances." This means they look at all the different factors in each case before they decide. Some of the factors that courts consider when looking at the totality of the circumstances include:

- Was the arrest in a high-crime area?
- What time of day was it?
- Did the child make any sudden or furtive hand movements so that the officers were worried that he had a gun?
- Did the child run?
- Was the child cooperative with the police?
- Did the child give a false name?
- How experienced was the police officer?
- Did the police know that the child had a prior record, or that the people the child was with had prior records?
- Did the police receive complaints from the neighbors? A radio call with a description?

Thousands of cases have been decided on the Fourth Amendment and thousands of law books have been written. This area of the law can get complicated, and it is always best to discuss the specific facts of your case with the child's attorney.

Frequently Asked Questions Regarding Motion to Suppress Issues

1. The police just rolled up and searched everyone on the corner. Marijuana was found on my child. Can they do that? It depends.

When is it okay to arrest? The police can arrest if they have "probable cause" that a crime has occurred and your child did it. If they have probable cause, the police can arrest your child and then search your child after the arrest. Probable cause to arrest means that the police have facts that would make a reasonable person believe that a crime was committed.

For example, let's say the neighbors have been complaining to the police for a while about the drug sales that are going on. The neighbors tell the police that the sales always happen at Eighth and Vine. If the police then set up surveillance at Eighth and Vine and watch your child sell to three different people, then they will have probable cause to arrest. Once they arrest the child, the police can go into the pockets to recover any other evidence.

When is it okay to stop and frisk? Even if the police don't have probable cause to arrest a child, they may be able to briefly "stop" and do a "pat down" on the outside of clothing. The police can do a stop if there is "reasonable suspicion" of criminal activity. The police may also frisk or do a pat down of the outside of the clothes if there is a reasonable belief that the child is armed.

Now, it is common knowledge that in some neighborhoods kids on the corner get stopped all the time. They get put up against the wall and patted down. In theory, this is only supposed to happen when there are facts that support it. If they didn't observe the child engaged in any criminal activity and they just go into the pockets and find marijuana, you may have a good motion to suppress. Discuss this option with your attorney. Even if you don't file a motion, it may help you in your negotiations with the prosecutor.

2. The school principal searched my kid's locker at school and found a Swiss Army knife. My kid now has a weapons case in juvenile court. Is there a motion to suppress here? Probably not. Students in school have fewer rights to privacy because the school has a legitimate interest in keeping children safe. As long as the teachers or the principal had a reasonable suspicion that your child was engaged in criminal activity, they can search the locker.

Unfortunately, many more children are ending up in the juvenile system because of something that happened in school. Where the incidents used to be dealt with by the principal or a phone call home to parents, now children are immediately arrested by police. This is largely a result of zero-tolerance polices that have been enacted in most school systems. (See chapter 12, "School Search Issues," for more information.)

6

Should the Child Take a Deal or Go to Trial?

TOP TIPS

1. Getting probation is *not* beating the case—the child will still end up with a criminal record.
2. Juvenile records count. The child's record will not automatically disappear when he becomes an adult. (See chapter 7 for more details.)
3. Take your time. Resist any pressure to admit to charges—make your own decision once you have all the facts.
4. Evaluate the strength of the state's case and the child's defense.

Fourteen-year-old John sat with his father in the courthouse hallway. It was the first court hearing since the detention hearing. John had gone to the attorney's office for an interview, but the attorney didn't have any of the paperwork from the case yet. The attorney told John he would get the discovery today, and then they would talk about the case.

John watched all the people coming in and out of the courtroom. Once in a while a person would come out and call someone's name. Finally, a lawyer named Kevin came out and called John's name. John and his father went down the hall with the lawyer, and stood near a window.

"I just got the discovery," Attorney Kevin said. "They are offering probation. I know we haven't had a lot of time to talk, but if you want to take this, you're going to need to let me know soon. If you don't want the deal, we can schedule this for trial."

John's father didn't know what to say. He knew that John had done some of the things he was accused of, but not all of them. Finally, John asked his lawyer, "Is this a good deal?"

• • •

Every defense attorney knows that working out a good deal is sometimes the best possible outcome for a child. But how would a concerned adult know if it is a "good deal"? When would the child be better off taking the case to trial?

In this stage of the juvenile court process, many different words are used interchangeably. For example, "pleading guilty," "taking a deal," and "admitting to the charges" all mean that the child is choosing to resolve the case without going to trial. Likewise, the term "trial" in juvenile court is the same thing as the "adjudicatory hearing" or "delinquency hearing." Finally, "disposition" or "disposition hearing" is the same as being "sentenced." (For a quick review of terms see chapter 1.)

PLEADING GUILTY IS FINAL

In most cases, it is extremely hard to undo or withdraw a guilty plea. It is not a decision to make quickly or under stress. In some jurisdictions, concerned adults and their children will feel tremendous pressure to take a deal not because it is the best thing for the child but because it is convenient for the court. Pleas are overused as a result of the enormous volume of cases that move through juvenile court. A variety of factors may push a child toward a nontrial disposition, but there is no guarantee of receiving a lighter sentence if he or she pleads guilty quickly.

Every child has the right to a trial, and it is at the trial that important due process rights are protected. Once a child admits to the charges, most of these rights are given up. The purpose of a trial is for the judge to figure out whether the child did the crime. At a trial the state has to prove that the child did it. Admitting to the crime (pleading guilty) means there is no need to have a trial.

Make sure you really understand the deal that your child is taking. I can't tell you how many times I've heard young people say to me, "I beat that case, I got probation." Getting probation does not mean you "beat the case." Getting probation means your child pled guilty, is under court supervision, and now has a criminal record. Frequently, when a child is first arrested, the prosecutor will offer some term of probation with or without conditions. Sometimes this is a good deal, sometimes it is not. Make sure you understand the future consequences of the juvenile court adjudication.

IS IT A GOOD DEAL? IMPORTANT FACTORS TO CONSIDER WHEN DECIDING WHETHER TO TAKE THE PROSECUTOR'S DEAL

Although there are hundreds of crimes that the child could be charged with, whether the prosecutor's offer is a good deal depends on the answers to the following questions:

1. How strong is the state's case?
2. How strong is the child's defense?

In order to answer these questions, you need to have all the facts. Has all the police paperwork (discovery) been reviewed? Has the investigation been completed? Have you considered pretrial motions? A child and his lawyer will not be in a good position to make a decision without a thorough understanding of the case.

How Strong Is the Prosecution's Case?

Once all the paperwork has been requested and reviewed, you will have an idea of how the prosecution will prove its case. You will know who the prosecutor's witnesses are and what they are likely to say. The next step is to evaluate the strength of the case. Consider the following:

Who is the victim/complaining witness? The complaining witness is the victim, or person who was "injured" by the crime. This could be the person whose car was stolen, or whose property was damaged, or who suffered some injury. Some cases are much more difficult to win because of who the complainant is. For example:

- Is the victim/complainant a police officer? A police officer may be the complainant if it is a drug case, or if the police officer was injured. If the case boils down to the child's word against the word of a police officer, the case will be difficult to win. If the only way for the child to be found not guilty is for the judge to say the police officer is "lying" or "mistaken," you have an uphill battle. The reason for this is twofold. First, police officers are really good at testifying in court. Even though they are not "expert witnesses" they are professionals at observing, reporting, and testifying in court. Because of their experience, police officers are often seen as credible. It is sometimes hard for the judge to find the police officer not credible. Particularly in juvenile court, where there are no jury trials, judges see these officers all the time, and there might be social and political pressure. Especially in urban areas where crime is high, it is difficult for the judge to go against those officers who risk their lives every day to maintain the law.

  Sometimes, there is no choice but to challenge a police officer head on because of ethics violations. This is just a word of caution: a police officer as complainant makes the case more difficult, and this should be a factor you consider when deciding whether or not to take a plea.

- Is the victim/complainant a very young child? If the answer is yes, this will make the case more difficult to win. If your child is charged with harming someone who is significantly younger/smaller than herself, as soon as the judge sees the two of them in the same courtroom, the deck will be stacked against your child. The judge's tendency to want to protect younger children from harm is a natural human response.

- Does the victim/complainant have a reason, or motive, to lie? Did he make inconsistent statements? Being able to discredit, or impeach, the complaining witness can be an important consideration when deciding whether or not to go to trial. If you have a reason why the complainant would make up facts or put the case on the child, you have a better chance of winning the case. Is the victim trying to protect someone else? Does he feel pressure from parents or the prosecutor? If bias or motive exists or if the victim made different statements at different times, you have a better chance at trial.

How serious is the case? This one is obvious. If the case is serious, it is more difficult for the judge to find the child not guilty. What is serious? In my experience, any time the victim ends up in the hospital it is serious. Of course, if it was just bruises and the victim was treated and released the same day that is not as bad as the victim who has a fractured vertebra and is in traction for three weeks. In terms of property, any damage over a thousand dollars is serious. For a drug case, if the child is charged with selling drugs, and money and drugs were found on him, it is serious. All gun cases are serious.

Will the victim/complainant show up? Consider whether the victim, because of her own criminal record or transient lifestyle, will come to court. Caution: as a concerned adult, you should *never* encourage a witness not to come to court because you can be arrested for obstructing justice.

Were there codefendants? There are three reasons why codefendants are helpful. First, if the other codefendants were much older than your child or were adults, there may be an argument that the child was influenced by them and therefore less responsible for the crime. The second reason having codefendants is helpful is that when multiple people are arrested the police did not think the incident was entirely your child's fault. This can help at trial and at disposition. Finally, if other people besides your child were arrested, you can learn valuable information about the likely outcome of your case by following the codefendant's case. What kind of offer did the prosecutor make to the codefendant? Was the codefendant successful with his pretrial motions? Assuming that two codefendants have similar backgrounds, it is likely that the outcome will be similar.

How Strong Is the Child's Defense?

Do you have a strong pretrial motion to suppress? As discussed in chapter 5, the reason to file a pretrial motion is to prevent the prosecutor from using certain evidence against the child. If the pretrial motion is successful it may be impossible for the state to prove the case. For example, if the child is charged with the possession of drugs, and after the motion the judge agrees that the police had no right to go into the child's pocket, the prosecutor can not use the recovered drugs as evidence in the child's trial. In this situation, without the drugs as evidence, there is no case.

Can the child testify on her own behalf? This is an important and difficult decision. There are obvious reasons why it might help for the child to testify and tell the judge what happened. Everyone in the courtroom is going to be wondering what the child has to say. In some situations it may be essential that the child testify, for example, in a sexual assault case where the child is saying that the sexual act was consensual, or in an assault case where the defendant is claiming self-defense. Unfortunately, more often than not, children are not great witnesses and can cause serious damage to their own case. In deciding whether the child is able to testify on her own behalf consider the following: Will the child make a good witness? How well does the child tell the story? Will she be able to look the judge in the eye? Is she articulate? When she talks does it seem as if she has an attitude problem or is angry? Can she describe what happened in detail? For example, does she know the names of the people she says she was with? Will she be able to hold her own against the cross-examination of the prosecutor? Are there any special education issues that will make testifying more difficult for her?

Finally, does the story make sense? This is often the place where adults fail to do their job. Because concerned adults love the child and don't want anything bad to happen, they tend to believe whatever the child says without question. Get real. Ask the hard questions. If it doesn't ring true to you, it won't ring true to the judge.

For example: The victim says he was attacked by a group of teens while he was riding his bike. The victim had some really serious injuries and ended up in the hospital. Your child (we'll call him Andre) was arrested. When you ask Andre what happened he tells you that he was there, but he didn't do anything. When you confront Andre for more details, he insists that he knows nothing: he didn't see what happened, he doesn't know who hit the victim, and he didn't hear what was said before the assault. Now, Andre might never tell you any more, but one thing is clear: Andre's story makes no sense, and he shouldn't take the witness stand and testify on his own behalf. How is it possible that he was there but saw nothing? More likely he saw everything but is too afraid to tell what happened, perhaps because he wants to protect his friends.

Does the child have a prior record? Be prepared. If the child has previously been found guilty in juvenile court, the prosecutor may be able to question the child about the prior case. Being questioned about past cases can be difficult for the child, so it is important that the child be ready for the possibility. A prior record does not preclude a child from taking the stand; it is just a factor to consider. This is an important discussion to have with the child's attorney.

Does the child actually have a defense? If you are going to go to trial, it helps to have a defense. Why should the judge find the child not guilty? If you have a strong defense and you can back it up with the evidence, case law, or witnesses, going to trial is a more attractive option. Common trial defenses include the following:

- Claims of innocence, such as: It didn't happen, it wasn't me.
- Alibi: I wasn't there.
- Self-defense: I only did it because I was defending myself.
- Merely present: I was there, but I didn't do anything.
- Insufficient evidence. This defense means that the state's evidence isn't strong enough to prove the child guilty. This is a very common defense that can be used in many ways. For example, let's say the child is driving a stolen car. When

the police try to stop the car, the child is completely cooperative with the police—he immediately pulls over, he doesn't run away. In addition, the car is being operated with keys. In this situation, even though your child is driving the stolen car, there is a good argument that he didn't know it was stolen. There is insufficient evidence to prove guilt given the circumstances. Why would a child who knew he was guilty be so cooperative with the police? This can also be used if the child did some of the things he was accused of but not all. For example, in a burglary charge, the child may admit to being on the porch, but not taking anything from the house, or in a car theft case, the child may admit to taking items out of the car, but not stealing the car.

• Incompetency. The child doesn't understand the trial process and is unable to assist in his defense. Note that this defense can result in delay until the child becomes "competent." For more information, see chapter 16.

Other Factors to Consider

How have things been going at home since arrest? If things have been going well since the arrest (for example, the child is going to school and abiding by the rules at home), the court is more likely to allow the child to stay in the community regardless of the outcome of the case.

What are the personalities in the courtroom? Remember, no matter what the law and the evidence, you are dealing with people, and it is important to understand them. For example, is this a judge who hates drunk drivers because his sister was killed by one? Is this a prosecutor who is particularly passionate when it comes to violence against women? Although I believe most judges and attorneys genuinely try to be neutral, they may have very strong feelings about particular crimes based on their own experiences.

Finally, what does the child's attorney's recommend? The child's attorney can be an important source of information in deciding whether to take a deal. The attorney may know how this particular judge responds to this type of case based on previous experience. Ask the attorney the basis of his opinion. If you don't agree with the attorney's opinion, you don't have to follow it, because the child has the ultimate authority in deciding whether to go to trial.

FREQUENTLY ASKED QUESTIONS

1. What Kind of Sentence (Disposition) Is the Child Likely to Receive If She Is Found Guilty? Will It Be Worse If She Is Found Guilty after Trial?

There is no way to know what a judge will do if a child is found guilty after trial. While most judges do not penalize juveniles for exercising their right to a trial, others will tell you that child will get some kind of break for "taking responsibility" and admitting to the charges.

2. Shouldn't the Child Just Take the Deal? At Least That Way She Knows What She Will Be Getting!

A guarantee is very attractive. People like certainty and knowing that the child will end up with two years of probation. In fact, in my experience, the main reason most adults encourage children to admit to the charges is because of the guaranteed outcome. After considering the above factors, you may decide a deal is the best choice. Just be aware of the future consequences. (See chapter 7 for more details about future consequences.)

3. What About Drug Court? Is That a Good Deal?

In some situations, your child may be eligible for drug court, or some other specialty court. The benefits of a specialty court generally include:

- Specialized treatment, for drug addiction, mental health, and other issues
- A judge who has specialized knowledge
- The opportunity to get the juvenile record expunged upon successful completion of the program

The potential problems include:

- In order to get into a specialty court a child generally has to admit to the charges and give up the right to a trial.
- If the child is unsuccessful, she will be removed from the drug court and given a new (potentially worse) sentence.
- If the child is unsuccessful, she cannot go back and have a trial.

4. What If the Child Wants to Admit to the Charges but Doesn't Like the Prosecutor's Offer?

The child always had the right to admit to the charges, whether or not there is an agreement with the prosecutor. The child can always admit to the charges and then the attorney can make a disposition (sentencing) argument to the judge.

5. What Does a Guilty Plea (Admission) Look Like?

The most important thing to know is that the child actually has to say she did the crime in open court. Wanting to take a deal for probation is very different from admitting that you sold the drugs or assaulted the teacher. Frequently, children want to take the deal but also want to hang on to their version of the story. In order to accept a plea from a child, the judge has to conduct a "colloquy." A colloquy is a series of questions the judge will ask the child to make sure he understands what he is doing and what rights he is giving up.

Typical colloquy questions include:

- Did you have an opportunity to discuss this with your attorney?
- Are you satisfied with your attorney's advice?
- Are you under the influence of any drugs or alcohol today?
- Do you understand that you have the right to go to trial?
- Do you understand that at a trial, you would have the right to cross-examine witnesses and present witnesses on your own behalf?

- Do you understand that you are choosing to give up those rights?
- Did anyone force you or threaten you to take this plea?
- Are you doing this of your own free will?
- You are admitting to the charges of _____ (At this point the judge may ask the prosecutor or the defense attorney to describe the facts of the particular case.)
- Is that what happened?
- Are you admitting to these facts because you are in fact guilty?

6. What Rights Does the Child Give Up by Admitting to the Charges?

By admitting to the charges, the child gives up the right to cross-examine the prosecutor's witnesses, the right to present witnesses, and the right to argue pretrial motions to suppress. The child also gives up most of his appeal rights.

7. What Would a Juvenile Court Trial Look Like?

Since courtroom scenes are so often the subject of television and movies, most adults and children understand the basics. Juvenile delinquency trials work the same as adult trials. A judge sits on the bench listening to the witnesses testify.

In many ways, a juvenile trial is the same as an adult trial. The same rules of evidence apply and the prosecutor has the same burden of proof. Just as in adult criminal trials, the burden of proof is "beyond a reasonable doubt," which is very high.

In every trial, the prosecution starts and presents all its witnesses first. The defense then has an opportunity to ask questions, or cross-examine each of the witnesses. Once the state presents all its witnesses, the defense can decide whether to put on witnesses. Because the state has the burden of proving the case beyond a reasonable doubt, the defense can decide not to put on any witnesses at all and just argue that the state has not met its burden of proof. If the defense does decide to put on witnesses, the prosecutor has the opportunity to cross-examine them.

8. Will the Child Have to Spend More Time in the Detention Center If He Decides to Go to Trial?

Maybe. If the child is currently being held in detention it is likely that he will continue to be held until the trial. How long it takes to have a trial depends on where the child lives. In many jurisdictions there are rules in place for children who choose to go to trial. Juvenile justice standards provide for an adjudicatory hearing within fifteen days of the arrest for children who are in custody and within thirty days for children who are not in custody. Remember, however, that even if the child is currently in detention the child's attorney can request that he be released. Whether a child should be in custody can be reevaluated at each court hearing.

9. Can the Child Have a Jury Trial?

In most states there is no juvenile right to a jury trial. This means that the trials are "bench trials" or trials that are just heard by the judge. The judge is the fact finder and will make all rulings on pretrial motions and evidentiary objections.

TABLE 6.1 Does the Child Have the Right to a Jury Trial in Juvenile Court?

YES
Although there is no federal constitutional right to jury trials for juveniles, these states allow jury trials for juveniles:
Alaska, Massachusetts, Michigan, Montana, New Mexico, Oklahoma, Texas, West Virginia, Wyoming
NO
A juvenile has no right to a jury trial, under any circumstance, in these states:
Alabama, Arizona, California, Delaware, District of Columbia, Florida, Georgia, Hawaii, Indiana, Iowa, Kentucky, Louisiana, Maine, Maryland, Mississippi, Missouri, Nebraska, Nevada, New Jersey, New York, North Carolina, North Dakota, Oregon, Pennsylvania, South Carolina, South Dakota, Tennessee, Utah, Vermont, Washington, Wisconsin
MAYBE
Under limited special circumstances, these states allow jury trials for juveniles:
Arkansas, Colorado, Connecticut, Idaho, Illinois, Kansas, Minnesota, New Hampshire, Ohio, Rhode Island, Virginia

Source: National Center for Juvenile Justice, *NCJJ Snapshot* 13, no. 2 (February 2008).

Note: All children tried as adults in adult court have a constitutional right to a jury trial.

10. Can the Child Get a Different Judge?

Usually not. The only way to get a different judge is if there is some reason why you think this judge might not be fair: for example, if the child had been arrested before and this judge put her on probation three weeks ago, you might believe that this judge will remember the child's prior record and will not be able to give her a fair trial, or if the judge knows one of the state's witnesses (for example, the victim is in the judge's wife's gardening club). If there is some reason to think the judge might be biased, your child's attorney can move to change the forum. *Caution:* If you move for a change of forum and your request is denied, you are then stuck with the judge you wanted to get away from.

11. What If I Don't Like the Judge's Decision?

No matter how you feel about the judge's trial decision, the judge will still be deciding whether the child should come home after trial. It is important to stay calm regardless of what you think about the outcome.

Second, you can appeal. This is a decision you should discuss with your attorney after the disposition hearing. Once things have calmed down and you know what kind of disposition the child receives, you will be in a better place to decide whether or not you should appeal.

ONE FINAL NOTE WHEN DECIDING WHETHER OR NOT TO GO TO TRIAL—ASSERTING INNOCENCE AND THE IMPORTANCE OF STANDING UP TO INJUSTICE

Sometimes, even when the facts are overwhelmingly in favor of the prosecution, it is important to go to trial. If the child adamantly denies the charges, it may be important for the child's perception of justice to go through the process, regardless of the outcome. Having his day in court, having a judge and the system listen to him, may be more important than the ultimate outcome.

In addition, if this case involves something bigger than the child, a larger injustice that needs to be addressed, such as unethical tactics by the police or a systemic bias in the system against a particular group of people, there may be very good reasons to take the case to court.

7

Will the Juvenile Record Go Away When the Child Becomes an Adult?

One of the most common myths about juvenile court is that the child's record becomes clean when he turns eighteen. This is not true. In most cases, the juvenile record will follow the child unless he has completed an expungement process. An expungement is when an arrest is erased from a person's criminal record.

In order to get an expungement the following steps have to be followed:

1. The child must first be eligible for an expungement (see table 7.1).
2. The child must file an expungement motion with the court.
3. The judge must grant the expungement motion. A judge can decide to hold a hearing in order to decide whether to grant the motion.

WHEN WILL THE CHILD BE ELIGIBLE
FOR AN EXPUNGEMENT?

The answer to this question completely depends on the circumstances of the case. If the child was found not guilty or if the case was dismissed, in most states the child will be immediately eligible for an expungement. However, if the child admitted to some charges, even if she only got probation, she may have to wait for a certain number of years before filing, or she may never be eligible. In some states, adjudications of delinquency for certain crimes are not eligible for expungement. Ever. You may need a lawyer to help you with this process. See table 7.1 to help determine if your child will be eligible for expungement.

TABLE 7.1 Will the Child Be Eligible for an Expungement?

Yes
• If the child is found not guilty of all charges
• If the child has charges dismissed
• If the child successfully completes a diversionary program
Maybe
• If the child was adjudicated delinquent of a nonserious charge
• If the child successfully completed a probation or treatment program
• If the child has no new arrests
Probably Not
• If the child is found guilty (adjudicated delinquent) for a serious offense, such as: – crime of violence   – unlawful sexual behavior   – arson, burglary   – weapons offense   – kidnapping   • If the child has many juvenile adjudications   • If the child has new arrests   • If the child demonstrates poor conduct when completing probation or treatment program

Source: National Center for Juvenile Justice, "Sealing/Expungement/ Destruction of Juvenile Court Records: Case Dismissed, Diverted or Informally Adjusted," *NCJJ Snapshot* 10, no. 8 (August 2005).

IF THE CHILD GETS JUVENILE PROBATION AND IS APPLYING FOR A JOB, DOES HE HAVE SAY HE WAS CONVICTED OF A CRIME ON THE APPLICATION?

Although professionals differ on this point, technically, a child found guilty in juvenile court is not "convicted"—he is an "adjudicated delinquent." So a child could say, "No, I was never convicted of a crime." However, if the employer then finds out that the child did have a juvenile record and was found guilty of a juvenile crime and chose not to reveal that, the employer may think the juvenile was lying. Again, this is why it is important to get an expungement if possible.

ONCE THE CHILD GETS AN EXPUNGEMENT, WILL THE JUVENILE RECORD SHOW UP WHEN SHE APPLIES FOR A JOB?

Once a person goes through the expungement process, it should not show up when she applies for a job. Let's say for example that your child (who was previously arrested) is now eighteen and is applying for a job. If she successfully completed the expungement process she doesn't need to disclose that she was arrested, because the expungement should have removed the arrest from her record.

Note, though, that in this age of technology, even if a child goes through the expungement process, the arrest may not be permanently erased for all purposes. The record may still be found by certain government agencies, including law enforcement and the criminal courts. In some legal proceedings, such as during sentencing for any crimes committed after an expungement, or in immigration/deportation proceedings, an expunged conviction may still be considered as proof of a prior conviction.

IF THE CHILD IS NOT ELIGIBLE FOR AN EXPUNGEMENT, HOW COULD THE JUVENILE RECORD IMPACT THE FUTURE?

Every state has different future consequences to juvenile records. These consequences can impact everything from getting a driver's license to lifetime sex offender registration (see chapter 20, "When the Child Is Charged with a Sexual Offense"). On the national level, there are also future consequences if the child is found guilty in juvenile court. Following are some frequently asked questions regarding federal consequences to juvenile court.

Can the Child Enlist in the U.S. Army
If He Has a Juvenile Adjudication?

Yes, under some circumstances. He is still eligible *after a certain period* for the following outcomes:

- Probation. If he is on probation he must wait until he successfully completes his probation before he can be eligible for the army.
- Court supervision of any kind other than probation (such as diverted disposition or adjusted disposition). If he is under court supervision he must wait until he is no longer under supervision *in any way* in order to be eligible for the army.

There is also a "maybe" category. He *might* be eligible (a waiver is needed) if he has been adjudicated of any of the following crimes as a juvenile—as long as he has not been convicted of or charged with any additional offenses within five years of his application for enlistment:

- Aggravated assault, assault with a dangerous weapon
- Attempt to commit a felony
- Burglary
- Carjacking
- Sex with a child
- Domestic battery/violence (as defined under the Lautenberg Amendment)
- Larceny
- Indecent assault
- Manslaughter murder

- Wrongful possession or use of narcotics or habit-forming drugs (excluding marijuana)
- Rape
- Sale, distribution, or trafficking (including intent to) of marijuana or any other controlled substance
- Terrorist threats including bomb threats

The answer is an outright no if he is adjudicated for more than one offense in the preceding list.

It is also no under some other circumstances. He is *barred* from the army for the following adjudications or delinquency:

- Prostitution involving a minor
- Indecent language to a minor
- Pornography involving a minor
- Convicted of murder
- Drug dependence
- Addiction to marijuana: history of chronic marijuana use or psychological marijuana dependence
- Two or more DUI offenses: two or more convictions of driving while intoxicated, drugged, or impaired in the three years preceding application
- Five or more misdemeanors: conviction of five or more misdemeanors that occurred preceding application. Examples of misdemeanors include:
  - Fighting or battery (no confinement)
  - Carrying a concealed weapon
  - Criminal or malicious mischief
  - Curfew violation
  - Damaging road signs
  - Disorderly conduct
  - Disturbing the peace
  - Juvenile runaway
- Two or more drug offenses: convicted of two or more separate charges of possession of any illegal drugs/drug paraphernalia within three years preceding application

Will the Child Be Able to Vote?

Juvenile adjudications do not result in loss of voting privileges.[1] But if a juvenile is waived into adult court and convicted there as an adult, the juvenile will face the same consequences of an adult conviction (losing the right to vote).

Will the Child Be Able to Work in Law Enforcement?

Maybe. Even if records of juvenile adjudications are "sealed" or "expunged" certain organizations and groups, such as the FBI, the military, CIA, and the criminal justice system, will have access to these records.

Will The Child Be Eligible for Public Housing?

Maybe.

- An owner of federally assisted housing shall prohibit admission to such housing for any household that includes any individual who is subject to a lifetime registration requirement under a state sex offender registration program.
- Public housing authorities have the right to evict families of delinquent children, even delinquent conduct does not occur on public housing property.[2]
- Eviction proceedings may be expedited in the case of criminal or drug activity.[3]

Will the Child's DNA Be Tested and Be Kept on File?

Maybe. In many states, juveniles are subjected to DNA testing and records can be preserved in DNA bank.

Will the Child Be Photographed and Fingerprinted?

Yes.

- Almost all states permit fingerprinting upon arrest.
- Almost all states permit photographing upon arrest (at least for investigative purposes).

- It is common to require transmittal and retention of finger-prints and photos to and in some central repository.
- A growing number of jurisdictions no longer require segregation of juvenile records from adult records in repositories.

Will the Child Be Able to Keep Her Driver's License?

Maybe. Most states have some type of suspension on driving privileges for juvenile adjudications.

NOTES

1. Robert E. Shepherd Jr., "Collateral Consequences of Juvenile Proceedings: Part I," *Criminal Justice Magazine* 15 (Summer 2000).
2. *Dept. of HUD v. Rucker*, 535 U.S. 125, 133–136 (2002).
3. 42 U.S.C. 1437d(k).

8

Disposition Hearing (Sentencing)
Asking the Court to Provide the Services the Child Needs

TOP TIPS

1. Show up. The presence of a concerned adult can make all the difference.
2. Come with a plan. Ask for services, but not too many. Overloading the child with too many obligations can lead to failure.
3. Pay attention to victim restitution. Unpaid restitution orders can have long-term consequences to the child and the parent.

Melvin's social worker knew exactly when things started to go downhill. It was clear to her why Melvin's grades had slipped from Bs to Ds, and why he had started hanging out with boys who got into trouble. It was all related to the death of his favorite uncle, Joe. Although Melvin was in foster care, his Uncle Joe came to visit him at least once a week—taking him out to see a game, or get some food. His Uncle Joe seemed to be able to reach Melvin and keep him on track, despite the loss of his parents.

When Joe was suddenly killed in a car crash six months ago, Melvin changed. He just didn't care anymore, about school or anything else. Melvin's social worker didn't mind that he was getting probation; she didn't want this one arrest to ruin his life. However, she hoped the court would order immediate grief counseling. Without it, she feared Melvin would keep getting arrested.

• • •

Disposition hearings are my favorite part of juvenile practice. This is the moment where the system stops focusing on the crime and starts focusing on the child and what she needs. In this phase, concerned adults are critical.

Regardless of how serious the case may have been, this is the moment when the court tries to understand what was driving the child's behavior. In my experience, it's often the serious cases that provide the opportunity for the most thoughtful and individualized dispositions.

For example, Samantha was an eleven-year-old girl who was charged with setting fire to her foster home. She started the fire in the basement, and by the time the fire department arrived, the entire house was destroyed. There was $70,000 worth of damage. Did she do it? Yes. Why did she do it? On the surface it appeared that Samantha set the fire in response to being upset when her older brother yelled at her. However, spending time talking to Samantha and understanding her past made it clear that she suffered from active posttraumatic stress disorder (PTSD) that had gone untreated. This PTSD was the result of extensive sexual abuse by her grandfather. At the end of the disposition hearing, the court stenographer was weeping for what Samantha had endured, and the judge did everything in his power to find the best possible nonsecure private treatment facility for her.

In another case, when I met Jose in a cell room he had three open drug cases. Each case involved the direct sale of narcotics to an undercover police officer. Did he do it? Yes. Why? Because he and his sister were living out of a car in North Philadelphia and he was trying to make some money so they could survive. They were living in a car because they had both run away from an abusive uncle who enjoyed watching Jose perform various sexual acts on his sister. When this information was presented to the judge,

Jose, although guilty of the drug sales, was placed in a therapeutic nonsecure environment. In addition, the judge agreed to expunge Jose's record once he completed the program so he wouldn't have a criminal record when he became an adult.

The link between childhood victims and subsequent criminal violence is well established.[1] Of course, many children in the justice system do not have this kind of trauma in their past. Still, it is important to think about why the child may be engaging in destructive activities. At the disposition hearing, if concerned adults can shed light on why a child may is acting in a particular way and be ready to address those underlying reasons, the court and the parents can become partners in positive change.

WHAT IS A DISPOSITION HEARING? HOW DOES IT WORK?

The disposition hearing is the same as a "sentencing" in adult court. It's where the judge decides the consequences for the delinquent act. It always happens after the adjudicatory hearing (either a trial or admission). Although the disposition hearing is the same as the sentencing in adult court, the purpose of this hearing is completely different.

Goal: Rehabilitation, Not Punishment

In adult court, the sentence is about punishment. Adults are given a definitive sentence, say six to twelve months, or two to four years. In juvenile court the purpose of the disposition is to rehabilitate the child. Because rehabilitation depends on the progress of each individual child, in many states the child is given an "indeterminate" sentence. The child will complete the sentence when she has been "rehabilitated." Sometimes this means completing a drug treatment program. If she does well, she could be done in six months. If she refuses to participate, juvenile court supervision could last for years.

When Does the Disposition Hearing Happen?

The disposition hearing could happen immediately after the trial or admission, or the child's attorney could request that the disposition hearing be held later. There are strategic advantages to each. If a deal was negotiated with the prosecutor, there is generally no reason to delay the disposition hearing.

If the details haven't been worked out, you may want to consider delaying the disposition.

Reasons for delay include:

- Allowing time for the emotions of the case to die down after a trial
- Allowing time for the prehearing disposition report to be completed
- Giving the child an opportunity to bring in additional witnesses to demonstrate community support

At the disposition hearing the rules of evidence are generally relaxed. The judge wants to hear from everyone, including the guardians, the probation officer, and the prosecutor, about what would be in the child's best interests. This is a great opportunity for concerned adults to be involved and to ask for any services the child might need, such as a mentor, anger management counseling, a special education evaluation, or trauma treatment.

WHAT ARE THE JUDGE'S OPTIONS?

The following options range from the least restrictive to most restrictive.

Probation

This least restrictive disposition is commonly used among juvenile court judges. Courts always have the option of imposing probation, regardless of the charge. Most judges tailor probation to the child by adding specific conditions. Conditions of probation can include the following:

- Daily school attendance
- Clean drug tests
- Weekly/monthly contact with the probation officer
- Curfew hours
- Community service

- Restitution
- Attendance at counseling sessions

If the child violates probation by getting arrested on a new case or refusing to abide by the conditions, the court can revoke the probation and send the child to an institution.

Community Programs

This option allows the child to live at home but provides more structure than probation. For example, there are community-based drug programs that a child can attend every day while still living at home. There are after-school programs that assist with homework and provide mentors. There are all-inclusive community programs that supervise the child from 8:00 A.M. to 8:00 P.M. and provide school and counseling. Each community has different resources. You can generally find out about community resources by talking to probation officers or other community leaders.

Residential Placements

There is a wide range of residential placement options. Some are so magnificent they look like a fancy private college complete with a large library and competitive sports teams (see, for example, http://www.glenmillsschool.org/, http://www .georgejuniorrepublic.org/). Others look just like prisons for kids, with barbed wire, locked cells, and metal cots. Some placements are privately run, while others are state run. Some programs are secure, while others are nonsecure (meaning a child could run away if she wanted to). Some programs allow home passes after a child has reached a certain "level." Other programs are specialized to particularly address the needs of girls, or sex offenders, or drug-addicted children.

HOW DO I MAKE SURE THE CHILD GETS A GOOD PLACEMENT?

Unfortunately, unlike getting information about a new car, it is difficult to get information about juvenile placements. The probation officer, child's attorney, or the Internet may be able to give you some information about the program. In addition, you (or the child's attorney) may want to ask questions of the program to make sure everyone is on the same page. For additional information see chapter 10, "When the Child Is Sent to Residential Placement." For sample questions to ask, particularly for children who need mental health treatment in placement, see the list of questions at the end of chapter 16, "Children with Mental Health Issues."

HOW WILL THE JUDGE MAKE A DECISION?
WHAT INFORMATION WILL BE USED?

Since the purpose of the disposition hearing is to give the child what he needs while considering the needs of the community, the judge will seek input from a variety of sources, including the following.

Parents/Guardians

Often, when children get arrested, adults have been having some challenges with the child at home. Sometimes parents are so frustrated that is may seem like a relief to have the child live somewhere else for a while. *Caution:* be clear about what you convey to the probation officer and the court. Your input carries tremendous weight. If the probation officer tells the judge that you can't handle your child at home, or that you are afraid of what your child might do to you or other siblings, the judge will be much more likely to order your child into a residential placement. If you want the child out of your home, be clear. If you are just momentarily frustrated but you still want the child to be at home, be clear about that too.

Probation Officer

Don't underestimate the power of the probation officer. I've been in courtrooms where the probation officer actually sits next to the judge on the bench. Prior to the disposition hearing, the probation officer may prepare a report. This report is based on conversations with the child, the parents, a review of prior juvenile court contacts, the success or failure of previous terms of probation or placements, school reports, and a review of the facts of this case. Although the judge may be inclined to defer to the probation officer's opinion about what is best for the child, as a concerned adult you are free to give input and present an alternative plan.

Prosecutor

The role of the prosecutor in the disposition hearing varies widely from place to place. In some jurisdictions he may be silent, letting the probation officer's opinion carry the day. In other cases, the prosecutor may want to represent the concerns of the victim. In situations where the child and the victim knew each other or go to the same school, the prosecutor may request a "stay away order" to prevent future contact. Some prosecutors may also request a "victim impact statement" to be read, making the court aware of how the crime has affected the victim's life.

Evaluations (Predisposition Report)

There are many kinds of evaluations that the court may order to prepare for disposition, including:

- Mental health evaluations (psychological evaluations, psychiatric evaluations, and neuropsychological evaluations)
- Competency evaluations
- Psychosexual evaluations

If you believe the child has some type of mental health issue, this evaluation may be very helpful. If you believe that an evaluation is necessary and the court has not ordered one, the child's attorney can ask the court to do an evaluation. In addition, if the court orders an evaluation and you do not agree with the findings, the child's attorney can hire his own evaluator. This can be a very complicated area. For additional information about children with mental health issues, see chapter 16.

WHAT IF I'M NOT SURE IF I WANT THE CHILD HOME?

Many parents struggle with whether it would be best to ask the court to place their child. It is a big decision—there are major risks either way. It is hard to know whether a residential placement will be good for your child. And it's hard to know if your child's behavior will improve at home after the case is over. I encourage adults who are on the fence to try more restrictive home options before asking for placement.

For example, if the court provides intensive structure, virtually eliminating free time for the child, the problems at home may disappear. Maybe a different school environment or a mentor would make a difference. Remember, if these home options do not work, and your child continues to violate the conditions, you can always go to the probation officer and request out-of-home placement.

WHAT IF I KNOW I DON'T WANT THE CHILD HOME, BUT I DON'T WANT TO HURT THE CHILD'S FEELINGS?

If at all possible, tell the child directly how you feel. For example, "I love you very much. You will always be an important part of this family. However, because of all the things that have been going on, I'm not ready to have you back in the house yet." This is extremely hard, but it is harder for the child to learn from his attorney, the judge, or the probation officer that his mother didn't want him home. Regardless of how you tell the child, make sure you maintain contact with the child while he is away. Cards, letters, and phone calls are very important to children away from home.

I WANT TO KEEP THE CHILD AT HOME. WHAT CAN I DO BEFORE THE DISPOSITION HEARING TO ADDRESS THE JUDGE'S CONCERNS?

In order for a child to be released to the community, the judge will need to know the following: where the child will live, who will be responsible for supervision, how the child is going to be educated, and what rehabilitation services will be put in place. These components are common to all disposition plans. If it is your goal to keep the child at home, spend time thinking through the following issues prior to the court hearing.

Where Will the Child Live? Who Is Responsible for Her Supervision?

If you want the child to return to the same home, be prepared to address what has changed since the arrest. Think about this as if you were the judge. The child was arrested; the judge is going to assume that there was some lack in supervision in the home. What was going on? Did the child become involved in a negative peer group? Did she begin missing school? Did she start using drugs?

What's Different Now?

Regardless of what happened, the question is what will the guardian do differently this time? If it is your desire to have the child return to the same home, be prepared to address how the structure of the house will be change to prevent further problems. For example, maybe you could change your work hours or ask other family members or neighbors to be involved to provide more supervision. If the incident occurred in the neighborhood or at the local school, you might consider having the child live with a relative so that he can be away from the local influences and attend a different school.

What Kind of Rehabilitation Services Will Be Put into Place?

The primary goal of the juvenile court system is rehabilitation. Rehabilitation involves giving children the tools they need to become constructive members of society, and it also means taking care of their physical and mental health. Consider the following:

- Employment. Are there any employment opportunities for the child to provide skills and structure? Even if it is doing construction with an uncle or babysitting, this can be an important part of the plan.
- Vocational training. Are there computer classes or automotive courses the child could become enrolled in?
- Community service. Can the child gain skills and give back to the neighborhood by doing community service?

- Treatment/counseling. Based on the psychological assessments, is some type of mental health treatment needed? Where in the community can those counseling services be obtained?

VICTIM RESTITUTION: WHAT EVERY ADULT NEEDS TO KNOW

Many judges order restitution as part of the child's disposition order. Prosecutors routinely offer deals that include a term of probation with restitution. Obviously, it is in the court's interest to make the victim "whole," but there can be serious long-term consequences to a child if she is unable to pay off the restitution. To protect your child, be aware of the following:

- If there are codefendants, make sure that the restitution is divided among them in an equal way.
- Review the victim's restitution receipts: don't just take his word for the damages.
- Make sure that the amount of restitution is appropriate to the child's age. In many jurisdictions the law says the restitution order must take into account the child's ability to pay. For example, it would be inappropriate to expect a fourteen-year-old to pay off $10,000 of restitution.
- Lifetime repercussions: If the restitution does not get paid off, it can be reduced to judgment when the child turns twenty-one. This can then be a lien against any mortgage she tries to obtain (or impact her ability to get student loans). In addition, in some states, the restitution payment becomes the parent's responsibility and is treated like a child support payment. Failure of the parent to make payments may bring the parent back to court.
- Final caution: Cases involving car wrecks. Pay particular attention to restitution if there was significant damage to a car. A car crash can result in thousands of dollars of restitution. Not only should you make sure you check the receipts, inquire about the victim's car insurance. If there is a $500 deductible, the child should be required to pay only the $500. If there was no car insurance, and the actual

out-of-pocket damages are in the thousands, you may be able to argue that your child should not be responsible for the entire amount. The victim should not be rewarded for driving without insurance by requesting that your child pay for all the damages.

HOW SHOULD I PREPARE FOR THE CHILD'S DISPOSITION HEARING? WHAT SHOULD I BRING? WHO SHOULD BE THERE?

The Right Attitude

Either the child admitted to the charges or the trial is over. Even if you don't agree with the outcome, now is the time for the child to take responsibility. Parents and children should always show respect to the court. For example, wear conservative clothes (such as khakis and a collar shirt, or a suit if the child has one), and don't chew gum while waiting for the case to be heard. In some situations it is appropriate to have the child apologize to the court or the victim, either verbally or by reading a previously written letter.

People Who Support the Child

The most important person to have at the disposition hearing is the parent or guardian who will be taking responsibility for supervising child. This person should be prepared to describe to the court how she will make sure the child's educational needs will be met, and how she will provide structure. In addition to the parents or guardians, consider bringing other members of the community to demonstrate support, including religious figures, employers, teachers, and coaches. If you can't get the people there, ask if they will write a letter on behalf of the child so that you can present that to the judge.

Recent Reports

If the child has been doing well in some type of pretrial program, has enrolled in a drug program, or has improved his grades/attendance in school since the arrest, bring documentation to show the judge.

Program Acceptance (to Avoid Incarceration
or Secure Placement)

If you would prefer that your child go to a particular program and you have information that the child has been accepted, this information will be important to present to the judge.

Having either a person to represent the program or a letter indicating the program will accept your child can be a powerful tool at a disposition hearing. Having the program you prefer agree to accept the child in advance encourages the judge to send the child there. This is an effective tool to challenge a recommendation of secure confinement or incarceration. Even if the recommendation is incarceration, as long as the child is in juvenile court, the emphasis is on rehabilitation. If your child's evaluation indicates special needs or treatment, demonstrate that the secure confinement does not provide for these services.

HOW LONG WILL MY CHILD BE IN PLACEMENT
OR ON PROBATION?

In some states, the child will receive a specific term of probation or incarceration, such as one year probation. However, in many states, children get what is called an "indeterminate sentence." This means that they will remain on probation or in the program until they are rehabilitated. For children on probation, the court will look at whether or not the child is going to school and doing well, whether the drug tests are clean, curfew is being obeyed, and whether there are any new arrests.

For children in placement, the program itself will generally have a level system to measure progress. While there is generally an "average" length of time for each program, say nine months, some children get out much sooner while others stay much longer. See chapter 10, "When the Child Is Sent to Residential Placement" for more about length of stay.

NOTE

1. James Garbarino, *Children in Danger: Coping with the Consequences of Community Violence* (San Francisco: Jossey-Bass, 1992).

9

How to Succeed on Probation

TOP TIPS

1. Take probation seriously. The child should complete probation and get out of the justice system as soon as possible. The longer a child is on probation, the greater the chance of probation violations.
2. Stay in contact with the probation officer. The probation officer can become your best ally against getting locked up, even if there are problems. Allowances are made for children who are really trying and who stay in contact with probation officers.
3. Pay attention to restitution payments—there can be serious long-term consequences for failing to pay them off.

Darryl was arrested while taking some CDs out of an unlocked car. Darryl decided to admit to the crime and was given six months of probation. Over the next six months, Darryl did not do the fifty hours of community service that the judge ordered. He also did not visit Ms. Jones, his probation officer, every month as he had been instructed, and did not pay the court costs of forty dollars.

After five months, Ms. Jones filed a motion to bring Darryl back to court. At the hearing, Ms. Jones said, "Your Honor, Darryl has been completely uncooperative while on probation. He disregarded all of the court directives. I am requesting that Darryl's original probation be revoked and he be given an additional one-year term of more restrictive probation."

Darryl and his family were stunned. Darryl had been arrest-free and had been going to school. His family just didn't think the other conditions were a big deal. Darryl's lawyer had no good explanation for why Darryl disregarded his probation conditions.

The judge decided to find Darryl guilty of the probation violation and added an additional one-year term of intensive probation. In addition to his original theft charge, Darryl now had a probation violation on his juvenile record.

"I BEAT THE CASE, I GOT PROBATION"

If the child is on probation, he did *not* beat the case. The child has been found guilty of a crime and now has a juvenile criminal record. How you proceed from here can determine how long the child will be involved in the juvenile justice system. As a concerned adult, it should be your number one priority to assist the child complete probation successfully. Successful completion of probation will get the child out of the criminal justice system.

This is a critical moment. Don't blow it by thinking it is no big deal. If you don't conform to all the details and requirements of the child's probation, the child may be in the juvenile justice system for years and years. This is not an exaggeration. I have repeatedly seen children with one simple term of probation stay in the system from the age of fourteen to the age of twenty.

WHY IS IT SO IMPORTANT TO COMPLETE PROBATION SUCCESSFULLY?

Probation violations have a way of keeping you stuck in the system and positioning you to be an adult offender. An article I wrote, "A Better Way to Spend $500,000," was the true story of a girl named Rose. When Rose was fourteen, she was arrested for fighting with another girl at school. First she was placed on probation, but she didn't complete it. Then, Rose was sent to a residential placement. She got out of placement and was placed on "aftercare probation," which she also violated by not paying restitution. Rose was then placed in another facility, and this time she ran away. When she was caught, she got sent to a third placement. The third placement was shut down for institutional abuse. From the time she was fourteen until she was twenty, Rose spent four and a half years in custody, all of which could have been avoided if she had completed the first term of probation. The indeterminate nature of juvenile court sentencing can create a nightmare situation for some children.

THE GOOD NEWS: PROBATION CAN BE A POWERFUL TOOL FOR CONCERNED ADULTS

The good news is that probation can be a powerful tool to get the teenager to comply at home. Many judges ask the parents directly what they want in terms of probation requirements, then instruct teens that if they don't do what the parents say, they will have to come back in front of the judge. So, if a child doesn't go to school, or is disrespectful in the home, all it takes is one phone call to the probation officer and the case can come back to court. You are in a more powerful position because you have the whole juvenile court system to back you up.

WHAT ARE THE GENERAL RULES OF PROBATION?

Each child's probation will be different, but the core requirements of probation are predictable. Even if the judge or probation officer does not specifically mention the following conditions, abiding by these rules makes sense:

- Go to school. Every day. On time.
- Be available for home visits by the probation officer.
- Abide by a reasonable curfew or abide by the curfew the court set. (A reasonable curfew for a teenager on probation is 7:00 P.M. on weeknights and 10:00 P.M. on weekends).
- No drug or alcohol use.
- No firearms.
- Stay in the jurisdiction (and if you are planning a trip out of state, make sure it is approved by the probation officer).
- Report any major changes to the probation officer (for example: if the child is in the hospital and has missed school, or the custody arrangement between parents has changed and the child now lives with father part-time, or if the child will be going to a new school).
- No new arrests.

WHAT ARE THE RESPONSIBILITIES
OF THE PROBATION OFFICER?

Probation officers are generally required to maintain contact with the child and to support him through the probation process. Specifically, probation officers should:

- See the child on a regular basis.
- Communicate with the parents.
- Ensure that child is following the rules.
- Provide resources to assist the child's adjustment to probation.
- Report on the child's progress to court.

Remember, the probation officer is a direct link to the judge. Whatever you tell the probation officer will get back to the court. Probation officers are "officers of the court." The probation officer is required to report back to the court. The probation officer is not an attorney who is going to keep information confidential. The child's attorney works for the child and it required to seek the expressed interest of the child. The probation officer works for the court and will relay all information he or she believes is relevant to the child's rehabilitation.

So, don't just vent to the probation officer. All guardians have bad days where they hate their children. Find a friend to talk to, or take a walk to calm down. If you tell the probation officer that the child is out of control, there is a good chance that the judge will use that information to increase the restrictions placed on the child or put the child in a residential setting. View the probation officer as a support, and as a direct link to the judge. Use the power wisely.

HOW CAN I SUPPORT THE CHILD
THROUGH PROBATION?

Since judges often tailor the conditions of probation to the individual child, it is critical that you understand *all* the requirements of the child's probation. Active adult involvement is critical in successfully completing probation.

- Understand the conditions and monitor progress. Is the child required to do any of the following? How can you assist in making it happen?
  - Community service
  - Program attendance (for example, anger management programs or substance abuse counseling)
  - Restitution payments
  - Court costs
  - Curfew requirements
  - Any other specific rules the judge ordered
- Don't miss appointments. Make sure you know when the child has appointments and assist her in keeping them. Keep a calendar that you review regularly, and adjust the family activities or work schedule to make sure the child is able to keep the appointments. Think about transportation and make sure to allow plenty of time for the child to get there. Nothing frustrates a court more than a child missing a scheduled appointment with a professional when there are so many other children on the waiting list.
- Stay in contact with the school to check on school attendance and academic progress.
- Stay in touch with the probation officer. Let the probation officer know if there are problems at home, in school, or in the community.
- Be aware of physical and mental health needs. If you think the child may be struggling due to physical or mental health issues, (for example, you don't have dental insurance and the pain in your child's molars is preventing her from focusing in algebra, or despite really good effort, her grades are still dismal), discuss this with the probation officer. Juvenile courts do have access to resources and may be able to address the underlying problems that are causing the school failure.

WHEN THINGS AREN'T GOING WELL

If you are doing everything you can as a supportive adult and things are not going well on probation, ask yourself the following questions:

- Are there too many probation requirements? If you believe that the child has too many requirements, report that to the probation officer. Sometimes, too many obligations set a child up to fail. It may be overwhelming to go to school, have a job to pay for restitution, do the mentoring program, and squeeze in community service.
- Does your child need additional resources to succeed? Most probation officers have access to resources that the court can order to assist your child, such as:
  - Behavioral/mental health support: testing, evaluation, and counseling
  - Academic support, tutoring
  - Skill building (vocational, educational alternatives)
  - Parenting classes
  - Mentoring

As I stated in the beginning of this chapter, doing well on probation is very important. The consequences of probation failure or a "violation of probation" will likely be an extended period of probation supervision with more restrictions or residential placement.

FREQUENTLY ASKED QUESTIONS

1. How Long Will Probation Last?

It depends on the jurisdiction and it depends on the child.

In some jurisdictions, judges give specific terms of probation, for example, a term of six months or one year. This means that the probation will last that long (unless there is a violation).

In other jurisdictions, children are put on probation without any specific time frame. In these jurisdictions, the probation will last until the probation officer or judge decides to end it. For example, let's say that Robert gets probation as a disposition without any specific time frame. This probation could last three months or three years. If Robert has done well for six months, a concerned adult could go to the probation officer and ask for Robert's probation to be terminated. If the probation officer agrees, he can bring the case back to court for a formal discharge from probation, or he may be able to discharge Robert from probation without going back to court.

2. I'm Not Sure If My Child Is Still on Probation.
What Should I Do?

If you are not sure whether the child is still on probation, check. You may believe that the child has successfully completed probation because you haven't heard anything from the probation officer in a while. However, if there was never a formal discharge, the probation may still be in effect. The longer probation continues, the greater the chance for a violation. Work with the probation officer to make sure your child's probation is terminated according to court records. If the probation is not terminated, any new problems that occur will be considered probation violations and could increase the child's penalties in court.

3. What If the Child Misses a Visit/Appointment?

Immediately notify the probation officer. As soon as you realize the mistake, try to make amends and reschedule. Missing one appointment or visit is not catastrophic and will generally not have any impact on the child's probation. However, if the missed appointment leads to weeks of silence for fear of facing the probation officer, it will lead to greater problems. Extended lack of contact between the child and the probation officer can lead to a bench warrant. A bench warrant issued for your child means the police can arrest her at any moment.

Probation is about being able to follow court rules and take responsibility. The court needs to know that the child will act responsibly when there are problems and do what is necessary to get back on track. One of the most common mistakes children make is that they don't report to probation and then they become afraid. Months go by without any contact between the child and the probation officer and when the child comes back in front of the court the judge is angry. When a mistake happens, fix it right away.

4. The Judge Ordered Random Drug Tests.
How Does This Work?

If there is any indication that your child has a drug problem, the court is likely to order drug tests. In some cases, every time the child meets with the probation officer, he will be required to pee in a cup. In other cases, the drug tests will be more random and the child will not know when or if he will be tested. Drug testing may seem invasive, but as a concerned adult there is nothing you can do to challenge it. Juvenile courts have a legitimate interest in identifying and treating addiction.

- What if the child refuses to submit to the drug test? The court will assume that your child has been using. A lot.
- What if the drug test reveals my child is using? Many children in the juvenile court system relapse at some point during their probation. It won't necessarily result in a probation violation. The question is how often he fails. Are the levels going down since probation started? What kinds of drugs are coming up positive—is it just marijuana or is it heroin or PCP? All of these questions will be considered. If the child's drug use is persistent (even if it is only marijuana) the court will look for an inpatient drug treatment program.
- "My child says he uses, but he is not addicted." When it comes to drugs, most children tell adults what they want to hear. Drugs are extremely addictive. Most children will need some assistance to stop. If you believe your child has a drug problem but the probation does not address it, talk to the probation officer about locating additional resources. For example:
  - Is there a community drug-counseling program?
  - Is there an Alcoholics Anonymous or Narcotics Anonymous group for teens in the area?
  - Is there a specialized juvenile drug court, where a child's record is automatically expunged once she completes the program?

Remember, kicking a drug habit is hard, and many children have used drugs to self-medicate in response to other trauma or pain. Finally, try to be patient and supportive: relapse is often a part of progress.

5. What If I Can't Afford the Restitution Payments?

Juvenile courts take the payment of fines very seriously. Failing to make restitution payments can have very serious and negative long-term consequences for your child.

The child may be ordered to pay to make the victim "whole." The negative consequences of not doing so are so severe that I would advise the family to help the child to make sure the restitution is paid off as soon as possible. Not paying restitution can keep a child in the juvenile system for years. As long as restitution payments exist, the court may continue juvenile probation, with the potential for violation. (See chapter 8 for additional information about restitution.)

If you are having a problem keeping up with the restitution payments talk to the probation officer; she may be able to help you create a payment plan that works. If the probation officer is unable to help, contact the lawyer who handled the child's case and see if the lawyer can provide assistance. The lawyer may be able to bring the case back to court to modify the restitution order.

Most importantly, don't use the struggle of restitution payments to create a probation violation. Stay in contact with the court and continue to meet all the other probation requirements.

6. What If My Child Goes to School with the Victim?

Do your best to stay away. Even if the court did not issue a restraining order, it is best to avoid the victim until probation is officially over. If the victim tries to have contact with the child, you may want to discuss this with school administration or the probation officer to get some guidance.

7. What If I Don't Like My Probation Officer?

Deal with it. It would be great if you liked the probation officer and he became your new best friend, but chances are that is not going to happen. One of the worst things you can do is get off on the wrong foot with the probation officer by challenging his authority. Remember, the probation officer is a direct link to the judge. Chances are that the judge has a lot of respect for this probation officer and would believe the probation officer over the parent or the child. You do not want to be labeled as a problem parent.

If, however, you believe the child is being harmed by the probation officer, continue to follow all the rules and call the probation officer's supervisor.

8. What If My Child Violates Probation?

First there will likely be a violation-of-probation hearing. At the hearing, the judge will decide what to do next. The judge could allow the child to remain on probation to try again, or, as a result of the violation, the judge could remove the child from the home and place him in a residential program. As a concerned adult, you should be prepared to tell the judge whether you still want the child home. If you do, what will be different this time to prevent further violations?

At a probation hearing, the best approach is to take responsibility and explain what happened without excuses or blaming anyone else. If the child is part of a community-based program, it will be helpful for the judge to know that the program is still willing to work with the child.

The outcome of the hearing will also depend on the type of violation. If the violation is missing a day or two or school, a hot urine test, or a missed appointment, the judge may be more inclined to give a second chance. However, if the violation is a new arrest for a serious or similar charge, the court is likely to put the child in a detention center until the new charges are resolved.

10

When the Child Is Sent to Residential Placement

TOP TIPS

1. Be supportive. Encourage the child to do well and don't talk about how much you need him at home.
2. Stay in contact. Inquire about the program rules and then call, send letters, and visit the child.
3. Be aware. Problems exist at some facilities. If you have concerns about the child's safety follow the guidelines at the end of this chapter and refer to chapter 17, "Institutional Abuse."

The judge looked down from the bench and said, "You may hug your child good-bye."

Gina looked at her son Charles, but he would not make eye contact. "Be good," she said, "I love you." She reached out to hug him, quickly, and then watched as the sheriff led him away. A few tears leaked from her eyes. Tears of sadness that this day had come, and tears of relief—at least she would know where he was every night instead of constantly worrying that he would end up hurt on the streets. Probation hadn't worked. This placement seemed like the only option.

Gina tried to hope, and prayed that this would be the fresh start Charles needed.

ENCOURAGE YOUR CHILD TO DO WELL

One of the primary factors in a child's success is the parent's attitude toward the placement. Many children who end up in residential placement can't actually focus on themselves because they feel they have to take care of their parents back home. Frequently, children have missed school to provide babysitting, care for an aging relative, or a buffer between mom and an abusive boyfriend. Whatever role the child played in the family, he will worry that something bad will happen when he isn't there. Reassure him that the family will be fine.

Regardless of how you felt about the judge's decision to place the child, try to stay positive and encourage the child to do his best. This could be a very positive experience for him.

This is an opportunity to start over. Regardless of how difficult things were back in the neighborhood or school, this is an opportunity for a new beginning. No one will know the child at the placement, and the child has the opportunity to make a great first impression. This is an opportunity to get away from a negative peer group. It is well established that peer pressure during the teenage years is intense. Teens fall into negative groups in order to create a sense of belonging, acceptance, or for protection. If a negative peer group has influenced the child's grades, interest in extracurricular activities, or motivation, this is an opportunity for her to break free of those influences.

Hopefully, the placement was selected with the unique needs of the child in mind. There are many specialized programs in the justice system. Whether it is a drug program, a program for girls, or a program for sex offenders, if there is a good match between the child and the placement, there is every reason to anticipate a positive outcome.

It is clear to me that for some children, a good residential placement is the best thing that could have happened to them. I have seen the graduation photos—the radiance on the children's faces as they pose in their graduation robes with their families: they are the ideal advertisement for juvenile court. The right program for a child can truly be a life-altering event, changing tracks from a life filled with criminality to a life of purpose. Some programs are wonderful. Unfortunately, not all of them are. As a concerned adult, it is important that you monitor the child's progress and stay informed.

FREQUENTLY ASKED QUESTIONS
1. How Long Will She Be There?

This is *the* most frequently asked question, and the answer is often frustrating. In some jurisdictions, a child will receive a specific amount of time at the disposition hearing. For example, in New Jersey, a child could receive a fifteen-month sentence. In that situation, a parent can expect that the child will be home no later than fifteen months from then. However, in many jurisdictions, the answer to the question "how long" is "it depends on the child." This answer makes children crazy and rarely gives the adults any comfort. The answer "it depends" reflects the reality that rehabilitation occurs as the child progresses. If the child is focused and does well, the child will progress more quickly. If the child refuses to participate (for example, if he won't talk to the counselor about why he uses drugs), the resistance can increase the amount of time spent in the facility.

Generally, when a child is committed, a program will have an "average" length of time. It could be six months or nine months or fourteen months. This means that it takes the typical child that long to complete the program. However, just because that is the average length of time, there is no guarantee it will take that long for your child. Children who fight with other children or who are disrespectful to their teachers will spend additional time in placement. Children who do extraordinarily well may complete the program earlier.

To understand how a child will progress in a program, do the following:

- Ask the counselor or the program director what the average length of time is.
- Ask about any level system. What competencies or skills is the child expected to learn at each stage?
- Ask for copies of any written material about the program.

2. Can I Visit?

Concerned adults should visit as frequently as the program allows. Contact with the outside world and reassurance that people at

home love them is extremely important to children in placement. One constant in every program I have visited is the importance children place on their friends and family back home.
Taped next to every bed are the cards and pictures that have
been sent from home.

Programs generally allow guardians to visit on holidays or after
a child has achieved a particular level. Each program has different
rules regarding visitation. Before you go, check the following:

- Are siblings allowed? Is there an age requirement?
- What kind of things you are allowed to bring?
- Are books okay? Magazines? Home-baked food?
- Is there a search procedure?
- What type of identification is required?
- How long does a visit last?
- Does the program provide transportation for family?

3. Can the Child Get a Home Pass?

In addition to allowing visits from family and friends, some programs allow home passes. This means that children may earn a
pass to go home for a specific number of hours or days as a result
of good behavior. For example, they may earn a day pass for
Thanksgiving, where they are allowed twelve hours at home
before they return to the facility.

4. What If She Doesn't Like the Placement?
Can I Bring Her Back Home?

No. She has been committed by the court. You don't have control
over when she comes home. First, allow time for the transition. As
I mentioned before, an adult's attitude about placement can
impact the child's perception of placement, so be sure to be
encouraging and supportive. If this is the first time the child has
been away from home, she could be homesick. For children from
an urban setting who are in a rural placement, everything will look
different and it may be hard for them to get their bearings.

Ideally, the court chose a program based on the child's specific needs. Be aware, however, that it is very difficult to change

placements once the child is there. Contracts, medical clearances, and transportation arrangements have been executed. There were court hearings and staff working to make sure the child got to this particular place. It is important to allow for a few months of adjustment before you come to court asking for a change.

Remember that in some situations it was the parents who demanded the placement because the child was out of control. If you requested a placement, don't change your mind after a few weeks and ask for the child back. Be clear with the child. Coming home without finishing a program is almost never an option.

Asking for a new placement could increase the length of time the child is away. Getting out of placement is contingent upon completing the program. The fastest way out is often just to deal with the rules. If the child doesn't like it and you ask for a change, the child may be perceived as manipulative. Even if you get your wish and the child gets a new placement, in many jurisdictions the time spent at the first placement doesn't count and the child will have to start the new program from scratch.

For example, let's say Billy was sent to the Happy Valley Boys' Ranch, which is normally a nine-month program. Billy spent four months there but hated it and asked for a different program. The court agreed and removed Billy from Happy Valley and sent him to the Mountain Top Boys' Facility, which is also a nine-month program. Once Billy got to Mountain Top, he would have to start the program from the beginning, which means he would have done four months at Happy Valley and still have to do nine months at Mountain Top.

Acting out will not get the child back home. Children are smart, and they will often figure out how to work the system to get what they want. Over and over I have seen youth misbehave in placement in order to be removed, only to end up at a more secure placement for a longer period. Behavior such as being disrespectful to staff, fighting with other residents, not participating in counseling, and taking other residents' personal items will usually lead to one of two things: a longer sentence and negative record at the original placement, or removal from the original placement to a more secure place.

5. How Can I Get Information about My Child's Progress?

At every stage in the process, let the court and the program know that you want to be an involved, supportive adult. Get a notebook and keep track of all the people who are involved with the child, and their contact information. Make sure you understand what each person's role is and how you can best support the process. For example:

- Who is the probation officer, and what is his office number and/or cell phone number?
- Who is the social worker or counselor assigned to your child?
- Who is the schoolteacher at the program?
- Who is the child's therapist? Does the family participate in the counseling?

In addition, you can get information about your child's progress by reviewing any reports and staying in touch with the child's lawyer.

6. What If She Runs Away from Placement?

Sometimes children run away from placement, either by finding a way to leave the facility or by refusing to return from a home pass. Either way, there will be negative consequences. If a child runs away, there is a good chance that she will be removed from that placement and placed in a more secure environment: think barbed wire. If the child is expressing a desire to run away, strongly discourage this and try to find a way to address what the underlying problems are.

When children run away, they generally run back to the people they know, either family or friends or the boyfriend they left behind. If the program notifies you that the child has run away and the child ends up in your house, call the placement immediately and inform them. By being cooperative and informing the program immediately, you will minimize the negative consequences. In addition, if you notify the placement right away you may be able to prevent the child from getting a bench warrant. A bench warrant is a notice to all law enforcement officers that if they see your child, they are required to arrest her.

Remember, talk to your child and try to find out why she ran. Maybe she ran away because she was being bullied by other residents. Maybe she ran because one of the staff members was sexually harassing her. Maybe she ran because of something she saw happen to another resident. If you believe that the child's safety is at issue and that she should not return, talk to the child's lawyer or probation officer.

Remember, the longer the child is on the run, the worse the consequences will be.

7. What Legal Rights Does My Child Have While He Is in Placement?

- Access to an attorney.[1] Children are entitled to access to the courts and an attorney while they are confined to placement.[2] If the child has issues while in placement that would best be addressed by an attorney, your first step should be to contact the attorney who handled the child's trial and disposition hearing. If that attorney is unavailable to visit with the child in placement, contact the resources listed at the end of this book.

- Grievance procedure. Every placement should have a grievance procedure. Having the child write the problem on a grievance form and giving it to placement administration is usually a necessary first step. Grievance procedures should be well defined. A well-functioning grievance procedure should respond to the child's problem within a week. Remember, whenever the child files a grievance, he should make sure to keep a copy for himself. This can be helpful documentation in the future.

Now, there are obvious problems. For example, if a child is encountering a problem with a staff member, it will be very difficult for the child to write down the problem knowing that the staff person is likely to find out, possibly get angry, and potentially retaliate in some way. In my experience, when I've investigated institutional abuse and I've asked a child if she has written a grievance, the response I usually get is, "Are you're kidding?" Still, it is important to use the grievance procedure, because when the child's attorney brings the issue to the placement staff, if the grievance procedure was not followed, the first thing the staff will say is, "We were not aware of the problem."

- Education. Placements take children out of their home, out of their school, and out of their neighborhood. The placement is responsible for the child's living arrangements and education. When children are placed, they still have all the same rights to an appropriate education that they had prior to placement. If the child has special education needs, those needs still must be addressed.

  As a concerned adult, make sure the placement is aware of the child's educational issues. If your child has been classified as a special education student, make sure the program has all the relevant documents including the IEP (individualized education plan). Children have powerful federal rights to an education. These rights do not cease when the child is placed. For more information see chapter 14, "Special Education Issues."

- Services ordered by the court. At the disposition hearing, the judge had the opportunity to order services for the child. For example, the judge may have wanted the child to get anger management counseling, trauma treatment, or speech therapy. Whatever the issue, the judge should have written it down in a dispositional order. The judge's disposition order is a tool to make the program provide the services. Work with the child's attorney. If the program refuses to provide court-ordered services, the attorney can file a motion to bring the case back to court for a hearing. At the hearing, the judge may inquire why the program refuses to comply, or order the child moved to a more appropriate program.

8. What If I Have Concerns?

- Talk to the personnel at the facility. If you have concerns about something that is happening in the child's placement, the first step is to talk to the personnel responsible for the child at the program. It is likely that the child will have a social worker, or a counselor, or someone who supervises the living space. Try to address your concerns directly to those responsible. Once you have done this, follow up with those individuals to see if improvements have been made.

In addition to talking to the facility administrator or the child's social worker/counselor, there may be a grievance coordinator in the facility who can give you assistance. You may want to follow up your phone calls with a fax to the facility administrator so that you have a written record of your discussions.

- Document everything. Whenever you talk to anyone, put it in writing. Get a notebook specifically for recording the dates of contacts and events and the names of people who are involved with your child while he is in the system. For example, if the child tells you that another resident of the program is threatening him, first call the program and speak to the counselor. In your notebook, record the time you made the phone call, who you spoke to and what they said. If the resident continues to threaten your child or if your child gets hurt, you now have a written record that you gave the program prior notice.

    Important information to document:
    - Your child's progress and setbacks. Always try to record: When you got the information (the date). Who gave you the information? What happened? Were there any consequences to the child?
    - Medical issues. Any time the child has to seek medical attention, either from the program nurse or at a local hospital record the following: What was the nature of the injury? How did the injury occur? What was the name of the doctor? Which hospital? How long did she stay in the hospital? What was the follow-up care?
    - Restraints, isolations, lockdowns. Document any time the child is put in restraints, isolation, or if his unit is placed on "lockdown" status. Record the following: How long the restraint or isolation lasted. How was it done? Was the child

held face down with a staff person on each limb, or was he confined to a chair? If the child was placed in isolation, how long did it last? What was the child allowed while he was in isolation (for example, did he have access to books? School? Visits by a nurse?) What was the cause of the restraint or isolation? Did anyone witness it?

- Medication issues. Was the child receiving medication before she went to placement? If so, is she receiving the right dosage? If your child was not taking medication before, and is being given medication now, make sure you understand what kind of medication she is being given and how much. Some placements overmedicate children in order to maintain control.

- Staff turnover issues. Unfortunately in some facilities there is frequent staff turnover. If the child had a good relationship with a therapist who then left after several months, it may be difficult for the child to reestablish a new relationship with a new therapist. Recording when a therapist left and who the new therapist is may be helpful in explaining why the child is suddenly encountering difficulties.

- Educational issues. Is the child receiving most of his instruction from the computer? Is the teacher special-education-certified?

• Contact the child's lawyer. The child's lawyer is in the best position to address the issues. Your lawyer has the power to bring your child's case back to court, write letters to the director of the placement, and visit the child to verify the information. Even if you haven't had any contact with the lawyer since the disposition hearing, call the person you remember. If this person is a contract (appointed) lawyer or a public defender, he may still be able to help. If you are unable to get in touch with the lawyer who represented the child at the disposition hearing, contact your local public defenders office and try to talk to someone in the juvenile division.

• Contact the probation officer. It is important to notify the probation officer of your concerns. The probation officer often may have the power to bring the case back to court for a review hearing and can inform the judge of your concerns. The probation officer can also visit or call the child to check in.

- Talk to other parents who have children in the same placement. If you are fortunate enough to know other parents whose children are in the same facility, try to gather information. Maybe they are having similar concerns, or maybe they have had other experiences with the program that could be helpful.

- Ask the child's lawyer or probation officer to schedule a review hearing. A review hearing is specifically designed to address postdisposition concerns. If there are problems at a placement, the judge can hold a review hearing to see if the placement is still appropriate for the child. A review hearing is a great tool. It is a place where parents' concerns and the child's concerns can be addressed. The judge is in a position to address those concerns either by a change in the child's status or by writing an order directing specific changes at the program.

9. How Do I Get Information About What Is Really Going On?

The best way to get information is to talk to the child. Visiting the child is ideal, because you can see how she is doing, rather than just hear her voice. Does your child seem calm or nervous? Is he sleeping, eating, and seeming to be generally healthy? Has she lost or gained a lot of weight? Does he have any complaints?

If you can't visit the child frequently, you have to rely on phone calls or letters. Unfortunately, letters may not convey the kind of information a concerned parent needs to know. In addition, clients may worry that their letters will be read by staff before they get sent.

In addition, sometimes a child's phone calls are monitored. If the child can only make phone calls with a staff member or counselor present, it will be difficult to get real information. A good strategy to overcome this is to first find out whether or not the child is alone in the room when he is making the call and then ask questions so that the child can give you yes or no answers. For example:

"Kyle, I'm going to ask you questions and I just want you to say
    yes or no, okay?"
Is anyone else in the room with you?
Is it a staff person?
Are you doing okay?
Are there any problems?
Can you talk about it?
Do you feel safe?
Have you seen anyone be hurt?
Have you been hurt?
Do you need someone (a lawyer) to visit you?

It will be easier for the child to tell you what is happening if you structure your questions this way. If you hear anything that causes you concern, use the tools mentioned earlier in this chapter and in chapter 17, "Institutional Abuse."

NOTES

1. Work product of Sue Burrell, Staff Attorney, Youth Law Center, used with permission. This work was previously presented at the National Juvenile Defender Summit, Washington, DC, October 27–29, 2006, at a workshop called Strategies to Keep Youth Safe in Juvenile Facilities.
2. The importance of postdispositional advocacy and access to counsel was recently emphasized by the National Council of Juvenile and Family Court Judges. See http://www.ncfcj.org/content/view/411/411.

PART II

Important Issues
and Special Populations

11

Transferring Children to Adult Criminal Court

TOP TIPS

1. Fight. Stakes don't get any higher. Don't waive any rights or agree to anything unless you completely understand your options and the consequences.

2. How good is your lawyer? Make sure the child's lawyer has experience handling this type of case. This is a specialized area and there are many things a skilled attorney can do to prevent a child from going to adult court.

3. Adult court is not good for children. Since the mid-1990s, more and more children have ended up in adult court. Studies show it is worse for children (because children don't get many services and frequently get hurt in adult prison) and worse for society (because upon release, youths who were sent to adult jails are more likely to commit violent crimes).

On the day of the incident, sixteen-year-old Nyeema had been in court, waiting for the judge to decide whether her baby's paternal grandmother should have more visits with her baby. Nyeema couldn't believe she had to go through this again. This was the second time the grandmother had filed a petition like this—the first one had been denied. The grandmother was constantly interfering: first by calling the department of human services telling them that Nyeema was an unfit mother, then by repeatedly calling Nyeema's job to the point where the boss let her go.

Nyeema knew that the grandmother wanted to see the child more, but it was just too complicated. After all, the grandmother was the mother of the baby's father, the father who was currently in jail for domestic violence against Nyeema. All Nyeema was trying to do was stay in school, work, and raise her baby.

So, when the judge ordered that Nyeema allow the grand-mother access to the baby twice a month, Nyeema was furious. And when the grandmother then walked over to her and got in her face, telling her "I told you. I told you I would get that baby," Nyeema snapped. She pushed the fifty-eight-year-old grand-mother away from her. The grandmother fell backward and hit her head on a metal chair, causing a cut that oozed blood on the linoleum floor; she left the court house on a stretcher.

The prosecutor charged Nyeema with aggravated assault and filed a petition to transfer her to adult court.

UNDERSTANDING THE BASICS

Children can end up in adult court in a variety of ways. The case may start out in juvenile court and then, after the prosecutor files a transfer motion, the juvenile court judge can decide to send the case to adult court. Or, based on the type of crime the child is arrested for, the case can start out in adult court, bypass-ing juvenile court altogether.

Legal Terms Used

Different jurisdictions use different terms when talking about sending youth to adult court. All of the following terms mean that the child will not longer be under juvenile court's jurisdiction:

- Transfer to adult court
- Waive (or waive up) to adult court
- Bind-over
- Certify to adult court, or have a "certification hearing"
- Decline

Rights of Children Who Are Being Transferred

All children facing transfer to adult court have certain due process rights as laid out in the Supreme Court case of *Kent*.[1] For these children, the stakes are extremely high. Because the potential sentence is years of adult confinement, it is particularly important that those concerned about the child understand the procedural safeguards and rights of the child. Children facing transfer have the right to the following:

- A hearing
- Representation by counsel

In addition,

- The child's lawyer must be given access to juvenile social records if requested.
- The judge must give reasons why he is in support of the transfer to adult court on the transfer order.[2]

WHY ARE SO MANY CHILDREN BEING SENT TO ADULT COURT?

A sociologist named John DiIulio looked at the rising crime statistics of the late 1980s (which were due in large part to the crack epidemic) and predicted that there would be a generation of children who would grow up to be "superpredators." These superpredators would be so lawless and so dangerous that the existing juvenile court could not handle them.

Fear swept through the country. State legislatures responded by making it easier for young people to be tried in adult court. Between 1992 and 1999, all states except Nebraska enacted new laws sending more youth into the adult system. An estimated 210,000 to 260,000 juveniles, or 20 to 25 percent of all juvenile offenders, were prosecuted as adults in 1996.[3]

John Dilullio was wrong, however. The "superpredator" never materialized, and crime has actually dropped every year since 1994. Research also reveals that the children most likely to be sent to adult court are African American children. Making up 16 percent of the general population, African American children make up 58 percent of the youth in adult prison. Finally, research reveals that sending children into the adult system is not only bad for the child, it's bad for society. Organizations such as the Centers for Disease Control and the National Commission on Crime and Delinquency recognize that the policies were misguided—when children who have been sent to adult prison get released they are more likely to be rearrested and engage in violent crime than the children who had just been sent to the juvenile system.[4]

HOW DOES A TRANSFER HEARING WORK?

State legislatures have developed a variety of ways to send youth to adult court. The following are the most common; you can go to the National Juvenile Defender Center at www.njdc.info to see the particular transfer structure of your state.

Cases That Start Out in Adult Court

- Statutory exclusion. This means that when children are charged with a particular kind of crime, usually a very serious one, a statute prevents them from being in juvenile court. For example, a child charged with murder or a gunpoint robbery is excluded by statute from juvenile court.[5]
- Direct file. Direct file states are similar to statutory exclusion, in that a statute prevents some youth from starting out in juvenile court. In direct file states, however, once in adult court the child may be allowed to present arguments to the judge that she belongs in juvenile court. After argument, the adult court judge will decide whether or not to send the child back to juvenile court.

Cases That Start Out in Juvenile Court: Juvenile Court Judge Decides Whether or Not to Send to Adult Court

Some cases start out in juvenile court and the prosecutor then files a motion to send the case to adult court. These cases may be called "waiver cases" or "certification cases." The judge will listen to arguments on both sides and make a decision. How much discretion the juvenile court judge has depends on the kind of waiver statute the state has.[6]

WHAT FACTORS DOES A JUDGE CONSIDER WHEN MAKING A TRANSFER DECISION?

Seriousness of the Offense

Probably the most important factor of all is the seriousness of the offense. A judge always has to consider the safety and protection of the community. The crime may not actually be as serious as it looks on paper, however.

When considering the seriousness of the case, ask the following questions:

- Did anyone get hurt? How badly? Did they go to the hospital? If so, were they treated and released, or did they spend some time in the hospital? Did they sustain permanent injuries?
- Were weapons used? If yes, what kind? If a gun, was it loaded? Did the juvenile have the weapon, or did someone else?
- Is this the juvenile's first arrest, or does he have a long juvenile court history? This is also an extremely important factor, and it makes sense. A judge is much more likely to give a child a break if there were not a lot of prior contacts with the juvenile justice system.

    If this is not the first contact with the justice system, how many other contacts were there? How many other contacts were serious or violent crimes? How many chances has the child had on probation or placement in juvenile court? When the child was in placement or on probation, how did she do?
- Was the crime against a person, or what it just property damage? A crime against a person is generally going to be considered more serious and less likely to be kept in juvenile court.
- How was the crime committed? Was the crime aggressive and violent? Was it well planned? Was it sophisticated?

If the answer to any of these is yes, it will be more difficult to make the argument that the case should be in juvenile court. Was the child alone or was he in a group? Many judges view solo actors as more dangerous. If the child was not acting alone, were the other people older? If so, the judge may believe the juvenile was influenced by the adults. Did it just happen, or was it planned for days? The longer the planning period, the more opportunity there is for a child to use better judgment.

What Is the Age of the Child?

This matters for several reasons. First, if the child is young, say under fifteen, the court can understand why she may have had poor judgment. Everyone can remember doing something really stupid when they were young. The older the child, the more accountable the court will hold them.

Secondly, juvenile court can keep a child until he is twenty-one. This means that if the child is young, the juvenile court system will have many years to work with the child. If the youth is older, say seventeen, juvenile court has less time to rehabilitate him.

How Strong Is the Prosecutor's Case?
Will She Be Able to Prove It?

Let's say the convenience store video caught your child on tape with a gun and a box of doughnuts. This is strong evidence, and the judge will be less likely to give the child a chance in juvenile court. If, however, the evidence is weak (the child has a strong alibi, or the witnesses are drug dealers who don't come to court), the judge will be more likely to send the child back to juvenile court.

HOW CAN I WORK WITH THE ATTORNEY TO PREVENT THE CHILD FROM BEING SENT TO ADULT COURT?

Transfer to adult court really is the end of the line. This is where the juvenile court "gives up" on the child, saying there is nothing more it can do. Since the stakes are so high, I believe in the "everything *and* the kitchen sink approach." This means doing whatever is necessary to make the court and/or the prosecutor see that this child is more than the worst thing he may have done.

If you can help the court understand how the child got here you may be able to prevent the child from staying in adult court, or be in a better position to work out a favorable deal with the prosecutor.

Tools to Keep the Child out of Adult Court

Social history report. Consider working with the child's attorney to create a social history report. This type of document is written after looking at all the court records, including school records and prior juvenile court interventions, and then interviewing the child, her family, and significant others. This type of mitigation document, presented to the court, can be extremely powerful.

A social history can reveal facts such as the child was abandoned by the father, or the mother left the child alone in the house for days at a time, or the family was so poor that it had to collect rainwater to wash, or the child lived in a basement with rodents, or she was teased or bullied in school every day. Many children who come into the juvenile justice system have had prior involvement in the dependent, or abuse and neglect, system. If a child has been in the dependent system, you can bet there are good juicy facts to use at a transfer hearing. Look at the records.

I've had the opportunity to use social histories that were so powerful the district attorney was close to tears when she read about the child's past. This doesn't mean the child is not guilty; it just puts the crime in context and may help the child get a favorable result.

School records. Make sure you get all school records to the attorney. Just as at the detention hearing and the disposition hearing, school records are important. However, in this situation, many of the children who are facing transfer will have terrible school records. Think about using them anyway. Was the child a special education child who never got services? Was the child just socially promoted or continually left back? Did the school fail to meet the child's needs?

Look beyond regular school: how did the child do academically in juvenile placement? How is he currently doing in the detention center? If you can point to any success, and the potential to succeed, it may be helpful in convincing the court to allow the child to stay in the juvenile system.

Family issues. Ask questions about the child's home environment. Are there addiction issues in the family? Did the child witness domestic violence? Did he spend time in homeless shelters? Did she lose a favorite brother to street violence? Any of these factors may have contributed to the child's current behavior. This is not the time to hide the family's dirty laundry. Although embarrassing, it could impact the judge's decision.

Acceptance at a juvenile residential placement. If you can convince a juvenile placement to accept the child, have someone from the program come to court and tell the judge why the program would protect the community and meet the child's needs.

Psychological evaluations. Consider hiring your own evaluation, even thought the court may hire one. A psychological evaluation could be important to identify a low IQ or other mental health issues that may have impacted the child's decision making.

MY CHILD SAYS HE WANTS TO BE SENT TO ADULT COURT. ARE THERE ANY BENEFITS?

Except in a very few limited circumstances, trying a child in adult court is *not* a good idea. Most teens are attracted to adult court because they think they can get bail. While this is true, the negative consequences of adult court are extreme.

First, adult prison is about doing time. No longer is anyone talking about rehabilitation and what the needs of the child are. Second, not only may the exposure to such a negative adult peer group put the youth in physical danger, but the older role models are the last people you want your child hanging out with.

Finally, once children go to the adult system they can never go back to the juvenile court system.

The *only* times it may be a good decision to agree to waive your child into adult court is if:

- The youth is older (eighteen, nearly eighteen, or over eighteen) and the crime charged is such that he will most likely get bail and probation (or a shorter sentence) on the adult side, *or*
- The option of having a jury trial outweighs other negative consequences.

Again, adult court is not a good place for teens. Make sure you and the child thoroughly understand the consequences.

NOTES

1. *Kent v. U.S.* 383 U.S. 541, 86 S. Ct. 1045, U.S. Dist. Col. 1966.
2. Randy Hertz, Marin Guggenheim, and Anthony G. Amsterdam, *Trial Manuel for Defense Attorneys in Juvenile Court* (American Law Institute/American Bar Association, National Juvenile Defender Center, 2007), 241.
3. D. Bishop and C. Frazier, "Consequences of Waiver," in *The Changing Borders of Juvenile Justice: Transfer of Adolescents to the Criminal Court,* ed. J. Fagan and F. E. Zimring (Chicago: University of Chicago Press, 2000), 227–276.
4. See National Commission on Crime and Delinquency Fact Sheet, http://www.nccd-crc.org/nccd/pubs/2006may_fact sheet_youthadult.pdf; see Report from Centers for Disease Control, http://www.cdc.gov/mmwr/PDF/rr/rr5609.pdf.
5. Even with statutory exclusion there may be some flexibility. If the state has a "reverse waiver" provision, even though the child is in adult court her lawyer will have the opportunity to argue to the judge that she belongs in juvenile court.
6. For example:
   - Discretionary waiver: the judge has complete discretion.
   - Presumptive waiver: the judge has less discretion. Here, if the prosecutor is successful in showing that the case

meets specific criteria, the child has the burden of showing why the case should not be sent to adult court.

- Automatic waiver: the juvenile court has almost no discretion. In this situation, if the prosecutor is able to show
  probable cause that the child committed the crime, the
  case is sent to adult court without consideration of any
  other factors.

12

School Search Issues

TOP TIPS
1. Children have fewer legal rights while in school.
2. School officials don't need a warrant to search a student's purse, backpack, locker, or desk.
3. Schools can perform random drug tests before allowing students to participate in extracurricular activities.

"Last week the vice principal brought my daughter into his office and asked to see her purse. Apparently other students were talking about my daughter smoking and it got back to the school officials. When her purse was searched, the vice principal found a packet of marijuana. Can he do that?"

Probably.

Children have decreased privacy rights in school. As discussed in chapter 5, the Fourth Amendment to the United States Constitution guarantees children freedom from unreasonable governmental searches and seizures. This provision does not apply in the same way to youth in schools, however. A search by a school official is still a search by a government agency, but because there is such a strong interest in making schools safe learning environments, standards are more relaxed and children have fewer privacy rights in school. Generally speaking, searches of students or their possessions are lawful if they are "reasonable" under the circumstances.

HOW CAN YOU TELL IF THE SEARCH WAS "REASONABLE" UNDER THE CIRCUMSTANCES?

A search is reasonable if it meets the following two conditions:

1. There are reasonable grounds for suspecting that the search would turn up evidence that the student is violating the law or school rules, and
2. The search was not more intrusive than necessary.

Ideally, factors such as the age of the student and the seriousness of the offense should be considered, but the conditions listed here make it easy for a school to meet the test. Information from a student that another student is selling/using drugs could be enough to enable the school to search. Information that a child has brought a weapon in his backpack could warrant a search.

FREQUENTLY ASKED QUESTIONS?
1. Don't School Officials Need a Warrant before They Go into My Child's Locker?

No. School officials do not have to get a warrant before they search. This applies to searches of students, lockers, desks, or other personal items. In general, lockers and desks are school property and do not belong to the students.

2. My Child Has to Take a Drug Test before Joining the Team. Is There Any Way Around That? What Will Happen If She Comes Up Positive?

There is probably no way around it. If she wants to join the team she'll have to submit to the test. Courts have held that it is okay for schools to insist on random drug testing as a condition to participating in extracurricular activities. This is true even when there is no suspicion that the child uses drugs. Because schools are responsible for maintaining discipline and for the health and safety of students, random drug tests have been allowed.

Each school district has a specific policy if the test comes up positive. In many of the court cases that have already been decided, the results of the test were kept private by the school and not shared with the police department.

3. What about Metal Detectors and Drug-Sniffing Dogs?

Courts have held that the use of metal detectors to protect and maintain safety is okay. In addition, dogs that sniff lockers for drugs are also okay, as long as the dogs are just sniffing all lockers and not those of individual students.

13

When Children Get Suspended or Expelled
School Discipline Issues and Zero-Tolerance Policies

TOP TIPS

1. Student behavior that used to get solved in the principal's office can now result in criminal charges.
2. School frequently use zero-tolerance polices on less serious behavior.
3. Check your school manual for details on behaviors that can result in charges.
4. Research reveals that school discipline is harsher on students of color.

Schools across the nation use zero-tolerance polices when dealing with student discipline issues. These policies can result in extremely harsh and absurd results. For example:

- A kindergartener was suspended for wearing a fireman's costume that came with an ax.
- A kindergartener was suspended for saying "I'm going to shoot you" to his friends while on the playground.
- A ten-year-old was expelled for bringing a paintball gun to show and tell.
- An eleven-year-old asthmatic student had his inhaler taken because it violated school drug policy.

- A thirteen-year-old boy was suspended when he took a knife from a girl when he thought she might harm herself with it.
- A fifth-grade Florida girl arrested on weapons charge for using a steak knife to cut the steak she brought from home to eat for lunch.
- A fourth-grade Pennsylvania girl who brought an eight-inch pair of scissors to school was taken out of class, handcuffed, and charged with a weapons offense.
- A thirteen-year-old Texas boy spent six days in jail after being asked to write a "scary" Halloween story for a class assignment. When he wrote a story about shooting up the school his paper was referred to the principal's office, and the principal called the police.

WHAT IS ZERO TOLERANCE?

The term "zero tolerance" means that there is a mandatory minimum punishment for a designated behavior. For example, a school will have a zero-tolerance policy toward the use of alcohol or drugs. In theory, any student who engaged in the prohibited behavior will be treated the same way.

After the Columbine High School shooting that left fifteen people dead, every state passed zero-tolerance firearms polices. Over the years, however, zero-tolerance policies have broadened. Today, the zero-tolerance policies of state and local jurisdictions include many more infractions than just firearms and can include infractions such as disobedience or disrespect.

However, unlike other criminal statues, under which a child has to have the intent to commit a particular crime, under zero tolerance the standard is more rigid. The student's intent doesn't matter. This "one size fits all" approach not only ignores student intent but also has been used inappropriately by school officials.

ISN'T ZERO TOLERANCE A GOOD THING?
WON'T IT KEEP MY CHILD SAFER?

On paper, zero tolerance sounds like a good thing. For example, saying that "our school district has zero tolerance for guns, weapons, drugs, threats, or disrespect" sends the message that a school will not tolerate any disruptive behavior. Unfortunately, although the original goal was to improve school security, zero tolerance has become a catchall phrase that has brought many more children in to the juvenile justice system.

By labeling every act a "criminal act" the system has lost any perspective on what actions are truly dangerous and worthy of punishment. Because of the rigidity of zero-tolerance polices and the inability of school officials to use common sense, the policy frequently results in outrageous newspaper headlines about children being arrested in ridiculous circumstances.

In addition to being arrested for minor school offenses, children are also being expelled and suspended under zero-tolerance policies. There has been a dramatic increase in school suspensions and expulsions in the past ten years. Suspensions are often the first step on a path of school failure and exclusion that leads many away from school and out to the street, where they will find trouble and a clear path to the juvenile justice system.

The children caught in this net are largely children of color, special needs students, and younger adolescents. The phenomenon known as the school-to-prison pipeline has been well documented.[1]

WHAT CAN A CONCERNED ADULT DO?

1. Be aware of the school polices. If you have any questions about whether it is okay to send in a cough drop or a knife to cut the birthday cake, ask the school in advance.
2. Be careful about what you sign. Don't sign anything that might give up your child's rights unless you are certain of the consequences. Make sure your child does not sign documents unless he or she has an attorney present.
3. Try to get involved early. If you know that your child is being bullied by another student and you are worried that one day your child will lash out and hit someone as a result of being a target, talk to the school about it. What are the school's policies on bullying? Make sure the appropriate teachers and guidance counselors are involved in any discussions. If the problem continues, send letters to the school board and

the parent-teacher organization. Keep copies of all letters
you send.

4. Use any due process protections afforded by the school disciplinary proceeding. Although these hearings are administrative hearings and offer fewer due process protections,
you should still be able to challenge the suspension or
expulsion.

Consider the following actions to get ready for the school disciplinary hearing:

- Bring an attorney or parent advocate with you to the disciplinary hearing.
- Meet with the principal of the school.
- Have members of the community write letters on your
child's behalf.

Remember, if your child has been classified as requiring special education services there are additional requirements that
the school must meet before the child can be disciplined.

NOTE

This chapter was prepared with the generous assistance of
Lili Garfinkel of PACER Center, Champions for Children with
Disabilities (www.PACER.org). PACER Center is a parent training and information center for families of children and youth
with all disabilities from birth through twenty-one years old.
Located in Minneapolis, it serves families across the United
States as well as those in Minnesota. Parents can find publica-
tions, workshops, and other resources to help them make decisions about education, vocational training, employment, and
other services for their children with disabilities.

1. See NAACP Legal Defense and Education Fund, http://www
.naacpldf.org/content/pdf/pipeline/Dismantling_the_
School_to_Prison_Pipeline.pdf.

14

Special Education Issues

TOP TIPS

1. The sad reality is that large numbers of special education children end up criminalized in the juvenile and adult delinquency and corrections systems.
2. Concerned adults(parents, advocates, educators) must be aware of the additional federal protections available for these children in the event of disciplinary charges.
3. Even if children are confined in a detention center or juvenile placement, they are still entitled to special education services until they are twenty-one.
4. The characteristics of special education children make them more vulnerable at every stage in the process, but particularly when being questioned by the police.
5. If you think a child might have a learning disability but he has never been tested, see your local parent center for help. (See the resource list at the end of this book.)

UNDERSTANDING THE BASICS

National Statistics reveal that approximately 32 percent of adjudicated children have special education issues. Individual state statistics have revealed that over 55 percent of the children in secure confinement are eligible to receive special education services.

If a child has been identified as eligible for special education services, there are additional federal rights that may be applied on the child's behalf. The federal Individuals with Disabilities

Education Improvement Act (IDEA) of 2004 mandates that special education children have the right to a free, appropriate public education (FAPE). The rights provided by this act can be powerful advocacy tools.[1]

WHY ARE THERE SO MANY SPECIAL EDUCATION CHILDREN AND CHILDREN WITH DISABILITIES IN THE JUSTICE SYSTEM?

When children who have disability issues are accused of a crime, their disability often makes the situation worse. For example:

- If they are questioned by the police, they may not understand their legal rights and are more likely to say things or behave in a way that makes them seem guilty. For example, these children might have more impulsive responses or not understand the question.
- If the children become stressed or frightened, their disability can interfere with the ability to listen, speak, and think. Stress might also trigger responses that make them seem not to care, or have what is called a "blank affect" or no expression of remorse. This could lead to negative impressions on the part of police officers and probation intake workers.
- If they become frustrated and act out or shut down, the judge at the detention hearing may assume they are hostile, dangerous, or offensively uninterested.
- Children with special education issues may not fully understand what their lawyer is saying. This may interfere with their ability to participate in their own defense or lead them to take pleas to resolve the case when they don't really comprehend the long-term negative consequences.
- Children with special learning or cognitive disorders may have more difficulty complying with the rules of a juvenile placement, which increases the likelihood that they will have more sanctions and be drawn deeper into the system.

What should I do when a special education child is arrested?[2]

As a concerned adult, you have critical information about the child that needs to be shared with the police, the detention center, the judge, and the child's attorney. Make sure to send information about your child's special education needs as soon as you can.

Make sure that you share the following information:

- The child's Individualized Education Program (IEP) or 504
- The child's most recent mental health evaluation
- Information about the medications she is currently taking (if your child is detained, provide the medication to the detention center)

FREQUENTLY ASKED QUESTIONS
1. What Should I Do at the Child's Detention Hearing?

Consider preparing a written statement for the court about the child's special education needs. If you suspect or know that the child has not received appropriate services through his school, contact a parent advocate and make sure this information has been provided to the court. It is important to let the court know that while you do not consider the disability an excuse for the behavior, this fact may impact his behavior.

Give a copy of the statement to the child's attorney. Include the efforts you have made in your school district and the community to address these needs. Be prepared to discuss what you will do differently as a parent to make sure further criminal involvement does not occur. If possible, have a teacher from the child's school or someone from the community present who can present evidence on the child's behalf, and indicate to the judge that the child is not a flight risk.

2. What If the Child Is Held in Detention or Sent to a Juvenile Facility?

You need to share information about the child with the facility as quickly as possible, including the following:

- Individualized Education Plan
- Medications

- Most recent mental health evaluation
- Any history of suicide attempts or severe depression
- Information about how the disability may affect the child's behavior

3. Am I Still Allowed to Participate in My Child's Special Education Plan Now That He Is Detained?

Yes. As a parent, you have the right to continued participation in your child's IEP. If you are not able to attend the meeting at the correctional facility, you can still participate in the following ways:

- By phone
- Asking questions about classes
- Obtaining copies of all educational records
- Agreeing or disagreeing, in writing, about the Individualized Education Plan

4. Can the Child Still Receive Special Education Services While Detained?

Yes. Your child still has the right to receive special services. These services can include the following:

- Individualized education programming
- Help with schoolwork
- Medication management
- Counseling
- Speech and language therapy
- Recreation services
- Occupational or physical therapy
- Transition services and vocational training

The right to these services continues until the child is twenty-one years old, and exists regardless of whether the child is in a boot camp, group home, residential treatment center, detention center, hospital program, or adult jail.

NOTES

This chapter was prepared with the generous assistance of Lili Garfinkel, from PACER.

1. For a more detailed discussion see Joseph B. Tulman and Joyce A. McGee, *Special Education Advocacy Under the Individuals with Disabilities Education Act (IDEA) for Children in the Juvenile Delinquency System* (Washington, DC: University of the District of Columbia School of Law, 1998), available at http://www.law.udc.edu/programs/juvenile/pdf/special_ed _manual_complete.pdf).
2. Adapted from materials from the PACER Center, www.pacer .org.

15

Does Race Matter?

FACTS
1. Minority children are overrepresented at every stage in the justice system.
2. One in three black boys born in 2001 will spend some time in prison.[1]
3. Latinos are thirteen times more likely to be incarcerated for drug offenses than whites.[2]
4. School failure is a primary pathway into the juvenile justice system. Research reveals that minority children are disciplined more harshly, resulting in a school-to-prison pipeline.

During the summer of 2007, the "Jena 6" case rocked the country. Thousands of people across the country rallied to speak out against racial bias in the adult and juvenile justice system. Thousands more went to the small town of Jena, Louisiana, to protest the case of Mychal Bell.

The case of Mychal Bell began in 2006 when a group of white students hung nooses on a tree on school grounds. Black parents and the principal wanted the students expelled. Instead, the board of education and school superintendent decided the white students would be sent to an alternative school for nine days and have two weeks of in-school suspension.

For months, racial issues continued to escalate in Jena. In December 2006, Mychal Bell, a sixteen-year-old black student, fought with a white student, Justin Barker, in the schoolyard. Justin was knocked out, got a black eye, and went to the hospital.

He sustained no permanent injuries. As a result of the fight, Mychal Bell was arrested for aggravated second degree battery and was transferred to adult court where he could have received a sentence of twenty-two years. The case became a national symbol for racial injustice. After Mychal spent a year in adult prison the court of appeals overturned the battery charge and ruled that he would be charged as a juvenile. Mychal was ultimately sentenced to eighteen months in a juvenile facility.[3]

You can't have a book about children in the justice system without addressing the overrepresentation of minority children, or "disproportionate minority contact." Anyone who has spent time in correctional facilities knows that mostly brown and black faces are confined within detention center walls. Some would dismiss this fact by saying that children of color are locked up because they commit more crimes. However, a closer look at the numbers indicates that the reality is much more complicated.

WHAT DOES "OVERREPRESENTATION" MEAN?
"Overrepresentation" exists when, at various stages of the juvenile justice system, the proportion of a certain population exceeds its proportion in the general population.[4] According to the National Council on Crime and Delinquency's January 2007 report:

- African American youth and Latinos are more likely than white youths to be detained for identical offenses.
- About half of white teenagers arrested on a drug charge go home without being formally charged and drawn into the system. Only a quarter of black teens arrested on drug charges receive that outcome.
- When charges are filed, white youths are more likely to be placed on probation while black youths are more likely to be put into a residential placement.
- African American youths are more likely than white youths to be charged, tried, and incarcerated as adults, and African Americans make up 58 percent of youths charged and convicted as adults and sent to adult prisons.

- At each decision-making point in the juvenile justice system, minority youths are disadvantaged. And there is a cumulative disadvantage as they travel deeper into the system.

The same report indicated that from 2002 to 2004, African Americans were 16 percent of the youth in the general population; however, African American youths were:

- 28 percent of juvenile arrests
- 30 percent of referrals to juvenile court
- 37 percent of the detained population
- 34 percent of the youth formally processed by the juvenile court
- 30 percent of the adjudicated youth
- 35 percent of the youth waived to criminal court
- 38 percent of the youth in residential placement
- 58 percent of the youth admitted to state adult prison

WHAT CAUSES OVERREPRESENTATION?

There is no precise answer to this question; research reveals the following factors have been determined to play a role in overrepresentation:[5]

- Police targeting patrols in certain low-income neighborhoods.
- Group arrest procedures.
- Policies requiring immediate release to biological parents.
- Location of the offense: white youth using or selling drugs in the house rather than on the street.
- Different reactions of victims to offenses committed by white and minority children.
- Lack of understanding of cultural differences. For example, in the Latino culture, it is a sign of disrespect to make eye contact with people of authority, but this lack of eye contact can be misinterpreted as lack of remorse or as indifference in the Anglo culture.
- Racial bias within the justice system.

UNDERSTANDING THE SCHOOL-TO-PRISON PIPELINE

Before children of color have contact with law enforcement or the justice system, they are in school, and research reveals that the school environment itself is a factor. Across the county, black children are disciplined more harshly.[6] For example:

- Nationwide, black students are suspended and expelled at nearly three times the rate of white students.
- In New Jersey African American students are almost sixty times as likely as white students to be expelled for serious disciplinary infractions.
- In Minnesota, black students are suspended six times as often as whites.
- In Iowa, blacks make up just 5 percent of the statewide public school enrollment but account for 22 percent of the students who get suspended.

SCHOOL FAILURES LEADS TO THE JUSTICE SYSTEM

Being suspended and expelled is a type of school failure. When children experience school failure, there are many long-term negative consequences. Young people who receive inadequate education disproportionately wind up in the juvenile justice system. Children who experience school failure are more likely to drop out, and dropping out of school drastically impacts their future options.

Research reveals that high school dropouts are more likely than high school graduates to be arrested and that 82 percent of the adult prison population never finished high school.[7]

WHAT PARENTS CAN DO

1. Talk to your child in advance about what to do if stopped by police. Engage in role play so the child can practice how to interact with police.
2. Make sure your child understands *his* rights, particularly the right to remain silent and the right to an attorney. Fill out the nonwaiver of rights form in chapter 2 and place the form in the child's wallet or book bag.

3. Be involved at every stage of the process. Develop a relationship with school administrators and teachers before there are any problems at school.

4. Go to the American Civil Liberties Union (ACLU) Web site, which has great resources regarding what to do if stopped by the police. See http://www.aclu.org/police/gen/14528res 20040730.html.

NOTES

1. http://www.childrensdefense.org/site/PageServer?pagename =Programs_Cradle_Juvenile_Justice.

2. http://www.childrensdefense.org/site/PageServer?pagename =Programs_Cradle_Juvenile_Justice.

3. Ultimately, the court of appeals overturned the battery charge and ruled that Mychal would be charged as a juvenile. Eventually, after the case became a national symbol for injustice, Mychal was sentenced to eighteen months in a juvenile facility.

4. And Justice for Some, Differential Treatment of Youth of Color in the Justice System, National Council on Crime and Delinquency, January 2007, http://www.nccd-crc.org/nccd/ pubs/2007jan_justice_for_some.pdf.

5. And Justice for Some, Differential Treatment of Youth of Color in the Justice System, National Council on Crime and Delinquency, January 2007, http://www.nccd-crc.org/nccd/ pubs/2007jan_justice_for_some.pdf.

6. Howard Witt, "School Discipline Harden on Blacks," *Chicago Tribune*, September 25, 2007.

7. John Hubner and Jill Wolfson, *Abandoned in the Back Row: New Lessons in Education and Delinquency Prevention*, Coalition for Juvenile Justice 2001 Annual Report, Coalition for Juvenile Justice, Washington, DC, 10. An overview of the report is available at http://www.juvjustice.org/media/ resources/resource 122.pdf.

16

Children with Mental Health Issues

TOP TIPS

1. Research indicates that most of the children in the juvenile system meet the criteria for at least one mental health disorder and that one in five has a serious mental disorder.
2. If possible, deal with the child's mental health needs *outside* of the justice system.
3. It may not be in your child's interest to highlight mental health issues in the court process. Work closely with your attorney to determine how to proceed.
4. For a quick guide to common mental health medications used to treat adolescents and their common side effects, see http://www.njdc.info/pdf/factsheetmeds.pdf.

By March, Kelly had become really worried about her daughter, Amanda. Typically a good student who enjoyed being involved in the school band and church youth groups, Amanda now showed little interest in anything. Her grades had gone from As and Bs to Cs. She seemed to spend all her time alone in her room, either sleeping or using the computer. Her appearance had changed too: she had lost weight, and now she wore a nose ring, dyed black hair, and black nail polish.

Kelly and her husband, Mike, tried to talk to Amanda, but she usually answered with one word. When pushed, Amanda would erupt in anger. In frustration, and feeling she had to find out what might be going on, Kelly searched her daughter's belongings.

She found pills and packets of marijuana; most disturbing, the computer revealed that Amanda had been communicating with an older man she had met online and was planning to meet him.

Kelly had no idea if this was a mental health issue or a typical teenage phase.

• • •

Sometimes mental health issues are easy to identify, for example, the rare child who has hallucinations. Sometimes a child's behavior, such as repeat fire setting, indicates a mental health problem. Most of the time, as in the situation with Amanda, it is difficult to know whether mental health issues exist and what exactly they are. The phrase "mental health issues" is one of those mushy terms that has been so overused it is almost meaningless. This term can run the gamut from the child who suffers from depression to the child who sets fires and abuses cats.

Many behaviors that look like mental health issues are typical stages in adolescent development—like moodiness, anxiety, or outbursts of anger. Other behaviors, such as drug use, challenging authority, and risk taking, are also normal developmental behaviors for teens. Unfortunately these same behaviors can bring children into the juvenile justice system and can be labeled as "mental health" disorders.

HOW DO I KNOW IF MY CHILD HAS
MENTAL HEALTH PROBLEMS?

In determining whether your child has mental health problems, consider the following:

- Is the child extremely irritable? Does he lose his temper easily?
- Does she have trouble making and keeping friends?
- Has the child previously taken psychiatric medications?
- Is the child withdrawn or anxious?
- Does the child have abuse and neglect or other kinds of trauma in his background?

- Is the child failing more than one core course or is she more than one grade below her age level?
- Is the child receiving special education services in the school program?
- Does she hear voices? Have flashbacks?
- Does he frequently use drugs?
- Has she ever engaged in self-harming or pain-inducing activities such as cutting or bulimia?
- Has he talked about wanting to hurt himself? Or tried to commit suicide?
- Is there a history of fire setting or cruelty to animals?
- Has there previously been a mental health diagnosis?

If you believe your child does have mental health problems, consider these issues when working with your child's attorney to make strategic decisions about the case. Mental health issues may have an impact at various stages in the juvenile court process.

IF IT'S NOT A MENTAL HEALTH ISSUE, WHAT IS IT?

It can be difficult to distinguish between mental health problems and the normal limitations of children, such as immature thinking and poor comprehension.

Immature Thinking

The limited capacity of a child in juvenile court may simply be a result of age. Immaturity can be disabling. Brain research clearly indicates that children's brains are still developing into the early twenties. As a result, it is common among teenagers not to think before they act and not to consider the worst possible thing that could happen before they take a risk. This is true of even the best student or young person with no behavior problems. Teenagers typically have such bad judgment that they are lucky if they complete high school without a serious car accident or other calamity.

Sometimes people treat teenagers' normal immature thinking as if it were a mental health problem. While some teenagers have a combination of mental health problems and immature thinking, most teenagers simply cannot think like adults. This does not mean they are depressed, oppositional, highly anxious, or have abnormal mood fluctuations.

Poor Comprehension

The younger the child is the more likely he will not understand some important legal concepts. Research has shown that even children without mental health issues have a difficult time understanding legal concepts before the age of fifteen. In addition, just because a teen talks like an adult does not mean he understands. Teenagers often have difficulty thinking through complex problems, do not organize the details of a story in a way that satisfies adults, or are reluctant to ask for help if they don't understand a question.[1]

FREQUENTLY ASKED QUESTIONS

1. Why Should I Get Help for Mental Health Issues Outside of the Juvenile System?

Ideally, adults should seek mental health services with and for their teenager outside of juvenile justice. In recent years many jurisdictions around the country have developed plans to improve how they identify and treat children with mental health issues. That's the good news. Unfortunately, the bad news is that many children with the mental health issues still get dumped into the juvenile system and get stuck there. They get dumped there for a variety of reasons, including a lack of accessible community mental resources and zero-tolerance policies in schools. Children get stuck because the care provided by the justice system often doesn't make them better. The juvenile system is a criminal system. It wasn't designed to be a mental health system. Sending children to a criminal system in order for them to "get help" for their mental health issues is risky. It may help, or it may make things worse.

2. How Will My Child's Mental Health Issues Impact the Delinquency Case?

If a child has some type of identifiable mental health issue, it may (or may not) be helpful to the child's case. At the very least, the child's attorney should consider the child's retardation or mental health issues in strategic case decisions at the following stages of the juvenile court process.

Pretrial police interrogation. If the child with mental health issues made a statement to the police, there may be a persuasive argument that the statement should be suppressed. Research is already clear that children under the age of fifteen who *do not* have any mental health issues rarely understand Miranda warnings. (See chapter 2 for more information about police interrogation.)

Trial. Generally, in order for someone to be found guilty of a crime, the person has to be "culpable," that is, has to have the intent to commit the crime. If the child has mental health or mental retardation issues, she may not have been able to form the intent necessary to be found guilty, or her culpability may be minimal if she was easily taken advantage of by others who encouraged her to do the crime.

Should the child testify? There are two ways to look at this, and you should weigh the pros and cons with your child's attorney. On the one hand, if the child has mental health issues, she may not testify well and may be easily confused during the prosecutor's cross-examination. On the other hand, it may be beneficial for your case to put the child on the stand so the judge can see exactly what her limitations are.

Disposition. Mental health issues should certainly impact how the court designs the disposition. A judge may order a specific kind of counseling or place the child in a specific kind of program. Hopefully, if the child has mental health problems, the child will go to a placement that is equipped to deal with those issues.

Note that most adolescent mental health problems are effectively treated while the child lives in the community, not in a residential placement. For example, most juvenile sexual behavior and most peer-related school problems respond better to outpatient treatment, according to research. *Caution:* If your child is sent to a placement, it is helpful to have the court draft a specific disposition order so that if there are problems later, the disposition order can be enforced.

3. The Court Wants to Do a Mental Health Evaluation. What Does That Mean?

Juvenile courts will frequently order mental health evaluations in order to learn more about the child's needs.[2] The following is a brief overview of the most frequently ordered evaluations:

- Psychological evaluation. This evaluation, conducted by a psychologist, will describe the child's mental and emotional functioning. The psychologist will administer tests or a developmental assessment that includes an intelligence test. Psychological evaluations will look at levels of depression or anxiety, intellectual functioning, recovery from trauma, development of thinking and identity, and communication skills.
- Psychiatric evaluation. This evaluation, conducted by a psychiatrist, should offer information about the child's history and development as well as information about medication management. In juvenile court, psychiatric evaluations are very brief (usually lasting less than an hour) and are used to determine if a child needs to be hospitalized or whether he would benefit from medication.
- Neuropsychological evaluation. This test is done by a doctor with specialized training in both mental health and brain functioning. This evaluation will offer all of the information in a psychological evaluation, plus give an analysis of the child's brain functioning and impairment.
- Psychosocial evaluation. This evaluation tells the child's story. A psychosocial evaluation can be conducted by any mental health professional (including a clinical social worker) and includes a thorough review of records and a number of clinical interviews. It differs from all the evaluations described previously because it usually does not include a formal diagnosis, battery of tests, and description of medications or analysis of brain functions.

4. Should I Be Concerned about the Court Evaluation?

Maybe. There are many potential benefits to screening children in the justice system for mental health issues. In an ideal world, these evaluations would be used to give guidance to the system so that the best decisions would be made regarding the child's treatment and rehabilitation. In an ideal world a mental health evaluation would be used to direct a young person and family to effective help outside the juvenile system. Early and comprehensive mental health screening by top professionals could be a great tool, but too often the child is punished for having mental health needs.

Current evaluation tools carry many risks. Depending on your jurisdiction, the negative consequences could include the following:

- Damaging information may be revealed that can make the child appear more dangerous. When the court orders an evaluation, a psychologist or psychiatrist employed by the court will be conducting the evaluation. Mental health evaluations frequently reveal sensitive information. Anything that the child says could be used to determine that he needs more "secure" placement, or make the court question the ability of the child's family to supervise the child. Remember, this is an adversary system. Think about what could happen when you take extremely personal information and give it to the prosecutor trying your case—who already thinks your child is guilty—and to the judge who will be making the decisions.
- The evaluation may not be thorough or accurate. Unfortunately, for a variety of reasons, court evaluations may not give an accurate picture of the child's needs. The court evaluator may not be highly qualified, may be biased, or may be dealing with a huge volume of cases. Some court evaluations are superficial and use boilerplate language, so the evaluations of many children read exactly the same. If the evaluator has to see fifty children every week, it is less likely that the evaluation will be individualized.

  Sometimes information can be missed. Let's take, for example, the boy who comes to court on a drug offense who is also missing some school and being disrespectful at home. Depending on the evaluator, this child could be diagnosed with a "conduct disorder," which basically means a teenager who has been misbehaving. A diagnosis of "conduct disorder" will tell you nothing about what is driving this young man to use drugs or miss school. It may be that there is a learning disability, or prior trauma. It may be that he is grieving the loss of a beloved uncle and is using drugs to self-medicate. A surface court evaluation will tell you nothing of the child's underlying needs and therefore the evaluation will not be helpful in determining treatment.

In addition to the commonly used "oppositional defiant disorder," the diagnosis of ADHD and bipolar disorder are also frequently given to children. These diagnoses can carry negative assumptions that the child is bad and always will be.

- Information in the court evaluation will become part of the child's permanent record. What teenager has not thought fleetingly about killing him/herself? But answering yes to "Have you ever thought about killing yourself?" may put a youth on suicide watch and give an elevated risk score that could be used against her later.

- Statements made during the evaluation could be used against the child later. Have you ever used drugs? This type of question can encourage the child to give incriminating information. This information can be used against the child in the future. If the court relies on this evaluation before the child's trial, it could damage the outcome of the case and end up pulling him deeper into the system. Most states do not have protections for children to prevent the use of these incriminating statements at various stages in the process.

5. Is There Anything I Can Do to Prevent or Overcome a Bad Court Evaluation?

You can't prevent a court evaluation, and it is in the child's best interest to be cooperative and answer the questions truthfully. However, you may want to consider doing the following:

- Prepare the child. Have the child's lawyer talk to the child in advance of the evaluation so the child knows what to expect, or better yet, have the child's lawyer sit with the child during the interview.

- Present your own plan. The adult and teenager can work with the lawyer to arrange to get mental health services to address the teenager's needs outside the juvenile justice and propose this plan to the probation officer and judge.
- Hire your own evaluator in order to prevent or neutralize a court evaluation.[3]
- Don't let evaluation alone determine placement or services. Try to design individual services, preferably in the community, to match the characteristics of the child.

6. The Judge Asked Whether the Child Was "Competent." What Does That Mean?

To be competent means that the child is capable of participating in the strategic legal decisions that impact the case. For example, does the child understand the role of the judge, the prosecutor, and the defense attorney? Does the child understand what it means to enter an admission?

Criminal defendants can not be prosecuted if they are not competent. This may lead a concerned adult to believe that "incompetence" is a good thing. However, even if a child is "incompetent" the court will generally respond by trying to make him competent or by waiting for them to become competent. Consider the facts of the case and the advice of the child's lawyer.

7. My Child with Mental Health Issues Has Been Sent to a Juvenile Facility. Is There Anything I Should Know?

Children with mental health issues have particular challenges when they are sent to residential placement. They may have difficulty understanding how the program works and what they have to do to succeed. The following is a brief overview of the kinds of additional issues they may encounter:

- Sanctions or negative discharge. A program agrees to take a child knowing that she has particular mental health issues. However, these same programs can be quick to discharge the child from the program if she begins to act out. This is true even if the child is acting out in accordance with her disability. Generally, it is a good idea to resist a negative discharge for the following reasons: first, because the child will internalize the failure and have to start all over again at a different program, and second, because given the negative discharge, the court may decide to place the child in a more secure environment.

- Medication issues. There are many medication issues to be aware of. Be proactive. Staff may knowingly or unknowingly overmedicate. There may be abrupt changes in the amount or kinds of medications the child is given. The program may lack psychiatric supervision of medication dosages. Ask questions, take notes, and consult with your family physician if you have concerns.

  All medications have possible side effects, some of which can be severe, including liver damage, diabetes, weight gain, slowed growth, agitation, or increased risk of suicide or aggression. Young people have to be monitored carefully for side effects and whether the medication is having desired benefits. Some medications require monthly blood work. Too often, instead of services being provided to address the needs driving the behavior, medication is used to control the behavior.

- Staff turnover. There is frequent staff turnover in many juvenile facilities. This can be particularly hard on children with mental health issues who become attached to their counselors. If you notice that your child is suddenly doing poorly, it may be a result of a change in staff and the loss of the child's sense of security.

Finally, if a child has mental health issues it is even more important to stay in touch with him if he is in placement. Remember, a child can still be represented by an attorney in this postdisposition phase. If you have any concerns, see the resources section at the end of this book and get in touch with your child's attorney.

CONCLUSION

Juvenile judges are often quick to find children guilty in order to "help the child." When you bring out mental health issues the judge has even more reason find the child guilty in order for her to get help. Focusing on mental health issues can also make the child appear more frightening to the judge, increase the level of scrutiny on the child's family, and increase the level of security at the placement.

If you can see a way to beat the case or get the child out of the justice system without opening up a mental health can of worms, it may be your best bet. The first question should be "does the child have a good defense?" If the answer is yes, the child's attorney may want to pursue that defense while the family tries to access mental health services in other ways.

NOTES

1. Work of Dr. Marty Beyer, used with permission. Dr. Breyer's work has previously been published in the following articles: "What's Behind Behavior Matters: The Effects of Disabilities, Trauma and Immaturity on Juvenile Intent and Ability to Assist Counsel," *Guild Practitioner* 58, no. 2 (Spring 2001); "Fifty Delinquents in Juvenile and Adult Court," *American Journal of Orthopsychiatry* 76, no. 2 (April 2006): 206–214; "Developmentally Sound Practice in Family and Juvenile Court," *Nevada Law Journal* 6, no. 3 (Spring 2006): 1215–1231.

2. Elizabeth Calvin, Sarah Marcus, George Oleyer, and Mary Ann Scali, *Juvenile Defender Delinquency Notebook*, 2nd ed. (Washington, DC: National Juvenile Defender Center, 2006), 41. Used with permission.

3. The child's attorney can hire an independent evaluator. The benefits of hiring your own evaluator are many. Generally, the evaluation will be more thorough and more individualized, and you can tell the evaluator exactly what to focus on. This evaluator may also be able to testify as an expert on the child's behalf at one of the stages of the process. There is the risk that since the evaluator was hired by the child, he will

be perceived as biased in the child's favor. However, this is a low risk for a well-qualified evaluator, and one that he should be able to overcome easily.

In addition, just because you get an evaluation doesn't mean you have to use it. You get to control what is done with the information in the evaluation. You may want to give a copy to the prosecutor and the court, or you might not. It completely depends on the circumstances of the case.

17

Institutional Abuse
Is the Child in Danger?

Unfortunately, I have personally represented many children who have been abused in juvenile facilities. First there was Rebecca, a girl who came to the system because of a fight with her mother and ended up being sent to a residential treatment program specializing in girls who had been abused. While in the program she was sexually assaulted by the night guard, who let himself into her room with his key. Next there was Lori, who, after an overdose, was sent to a recovery hospital where a staff member said he would give her cigarettes and phone calls in exchange for sexual favors. Then there was Michael, who, while he was in secure confinement, endured restraints lasting ten hours (with guards on each limb). Seventeen-year-old Walter's restraints were so severe that he died in the facility.

ABUSE IN JUVENILE FACILITIES IS A NATIONAL PROBLEM
Every year, all over the country children are committed by courts to placements for treatment where they are subsequently abused.

Statistics of abuse and mistreatment in youth correctional facilities can be hard to measure. However, in 2004 there were 2,821 reports of sexual violence against youth and 26 deaths of youth in facilities.[1] At the beginning of 2007, news of the conditions in the facilities of the Texas Youth Commission served as an example, with widespread abuses that had gone ignored for years.[2]

FACTORS THAT CONTRIBUTE TO INSTITUTIONAL ABUSE

Many factors contribute to institutional abuse, including the following:

- Children are often placed far from home and lack access to family.
- Children lack access to attorneys while in placement. This occurs because most children are poor and are represented by the public defender's office. These offices often have large caseloads, and staying in touch with children once they are placed is generally a low priority.
- Facility inspectors lack effective tools to track problems and complaints.
- Judges and probation officers responsible for placing the children in facilities are unaware of problems. Even when reports are made, information is not cataloged so that it is easy to find.
- Private for-profit facilities hire unqualified staff in order to control costs. Staff often lacks training and supervision.
- Overcrowded facilities exacerbate any existing problems.

BUILT-IN DISINCENTIVES:
WHY CHILDREN DON'T REPORT PROBLEMS

Think about it this way. You are a teen in placement. You know that your counselor will be talking to your probation officer, who will be talking to your judge. If the program gets to decide when you go home, do you really want to complain about anything? Let's say you do complain about the behavior of a particular staff person. What if they don't believe you? Will they retaliate? Will they report to the probation officer that your "adjustment has been problematic" to make you stay longer? Will they make your life miserable for snitching?

There are many disincentives for children to report problems in facilities. These disincentives include:

- Fear of retaliation
- Fear that they won't be believed
- Fear that they will have to stay longer
- Fear that they will be negatively discharged and have to start over somewhere else

As discussed in prior chapters, in some parts of the country children do not receive a sentence but rather must stay in the facility until staff deems they have been "rehabilitated." This structure gives tremendous discretion to the facility, since the program gets to decide when and if children are ready to be released.

INFORMATION ABOUT PROGRAMS IS HARD TO GET

It is hard to get good information about programs for children in the juvenile system. In many ways the programs all look alike and use the same terms. Existing statistics rarely allow for program comparison. It is not like shopping for colleges or a new car: programs generally do not reveal useful information to the public.

If, as a concerned adult, you have the opportunity to ask questions about the program, you might inquire about the following:

- How often does a child meet with an individual counselor, and for how long?
- What is the educational level of the counselor? (Does she have an associate's degree in psychology from the local community college, or is she a psychologist with an advanced degree and experience?)
- How many teachers are special education–certified?
- What percentage of the staff have college degrees?
- How many of the children went on to graduate from high school or college after completing the program?
- How many children get rearrested within a year of their release?
- How many complaints have been filed against the facility, and for what?

WHAT CAN CONCERNED ADULTS DO
IF THEY ARE WORRIED ABOUT ABUSE?

Sue Burrell of the Youth Law Center in California has developed the following tips for concerned adults. Different strategies can be used depending on the seriousness of the situation. With each of these strategies, *always make sure to tell the child what you plan to do, and make sure he wants you to proceed.*[3]

1. *Make a phone call to the facility administrator.* Using the telephone is a good strategy when there is something specific you want to accomplish, such as getting the facility to take your child to a doctor, or arrange a personal visit with someone not on the visiting list. Keep a record of the person(s) you speak with, the date, and what was said. Also ask for a return phone call or written response when any requested action is carried out.

2. *Contact your lawyer.* Children have the right to access to counsel while they are in a juvenile placement.

3. *Send a fax to the facility administrator.* If the request is one with some urgency, such as a situation where you need to have a mental health clinician check into a child's mental health status, you may want to fax a written request asking the administrator to investigate and take prompt appropriate action to address the situation. Faxing has the added advantage of giving you a written record of the request. Keep copies of the successful fax. You could also use e-mail, but because administrators get a huge number of e-mails, faxes stand out better as communications calling for a response.

4. *Contact the ombudsperson or grievance coordinator.* If the request has to do with some sort of relationship issue (for example, trouble with a particular staff member) or incident in the facility, you may want to call the ombudsperson, or if there isn't one, contact the grievance coordinator for advice.

5. *Have the child's attorney write a letter to the facility administrator.* If the issue involves issues that are very serious, or your less formal attempts to resolve them fail, have the child's attorney

write a letter to the administrator of the facility asking for investigation or specific action, outlining what you know about the matter, and asking for a prompt written response.

6. *Notify the licensing or regulatory agency.* If the facility or placement is licensed, or there is a regulatory agency, there may be a complaint process for investigation and action in individual cases. For example, group homes in California are licensed by the California Department of Social Services. Children may file complaints through the Foster Care Ombudsman (http://www.dss.cahwnet.gov/pdf/pub379.pdf), and any person may file complaints directly with the agency. Typically, state law requires investigation and response in a specified period of time, and complaints are retained in the licensing file.

7. *Make a child abuse report.* Most states have provisions for filing complaints in relation to physical or sexual abuse of children, and this includes abuse by staff in facilities or by law enforcement officers. These reports may be confidentially filed, and the child welfare agency in the jurisdiction must respond to them.

8. *Involve specialty advocates for assistance.* A disproportionate number of youth in juvenile justice have disabilities qualifying them for special education services or calling for services for developmental disabilities or mental health conditions. Accordingly, in the individual cases where you need help, contact your local Protection and Advocacy (P & A) office or other agencies that provide educational, developmental disabilities, and mental health advocacy services.

9. *Contact the Civil Rights Division of the U.S. Department of Justice.* The Civil Rights of Institutionalized Persons Act (CRIPA) gives the Civil Rights Division of the U.S. Department of Justice (DOJ) power to bring action against the state if civil rights are violated in publicly operated facilities. If you receive information that indicates abuse, contact the Special Litigation Section, Civil Rights Division, U.S. Department of Justice, P.O. Box 66400, Washington, DC 20035–6400, (202) 514–6255 (Web site)www.usdoj.gov/crt/split/juveniles.htm.

NOTES

1. Rashida Edmondson-Penny, "Why It's Important to Know Your Rights: A Young People's Guide to Juvenile Delinquency Court" (Gault at 40 Campaign publication supported by the National Juvenile Defender Center), 5, kyr_booklet.pdf. Information about Gault at 40 is available at www.gaultat40.info/knowyour rights.php.

2. Sylvia Moreno, "In Texas, Scandals Rock Juvenile Justice System; Hundreds to Be Released as State Looks at Abuse Allegations and Sentencing Policies," *Washington Post*, April 5, 2007, A3.

3. Sue Burrell, Esq., Youth Law Center, San Francisco California. Work previously presented at Beyond the Bench XIX conference, San Francisco, December 11, 2007, at a workshop titled "Solving Conditions of Confinement Problems for Youth in the Delinquency System: Self-Help for the Practitioners."

18

The Special Needs of Lesbian, Gay, Bisexual, and Transgender Youth

TOP TIPS

1. Be aware. Lesbian, gay, bisexual, and transgender (LGBT) youth frequently face discrimination, harassment, and isolation while in juvenile facilities.
2. Stay in contact with the child and monitor his treatment while in any kind of juvenile facility.
3. If you suspect institutional abuse, follow the guidelines in chapter 17.

A case from Hawaii, heard by the United States district court in 2006, illustrates the kinds of issues lesbian, gay, bisexual, and transgender (LGBT) children face while confined in facilities. In this case, three teen residents—a gay girl, a boy perceived to be gay, and a transgender girl—testified to the routine practice of staff and other residents verbally abusing children who were perceived as LGBT. Girls were called "butchie" or "playing the bull" or "fucking cunts." The boy was called "faggot" and "dick sucker" on a daily basis. The staff did nothing to prevent the verbal abuse.

During a group counseling session, the gay teen was told that she was "disgusting" and the other wards were allowed to develop the punishment for her and another girl with whom she had a relationship. At one point, the transgender girl was transferred from the girls' unit to the boys' unit, where she was subject to threats of rape and assault. Additionally, both girls were denied permission to speak to their attorneys. When the boy wrote to the administrator, telling him that he might harm himself as a way to end the harassment, his letter was ignored for four days, leaving him at risk without any intervention.

In addition to the verbal abuse and staff ignorance, the children who identified as LGBT were threatened with physical and sexual assaults and were subjected to various forms of unwanted sexual touching. Again, the supervisors of the Hawaii Youth Correctional Facility were aware of the behavior and did nothing to prevent it. When the staff did document incidents, disciplinary measures were either nonexistent or were ineffective in stopping further harassment of these teens.

INCREASED DANGERS FOR LBGT CHILDREN

The remedy chosen by the Hawaii Youth Correctional Facility was isolation of the victimized teens. While in isolation, the children were prevented from making phone calls or writing letters. They were allowed one hour of solo recreation and one shower per day.[1]

Children who are questioning their sexual orientation or who identify as lesbian, gay, bisexual, or transgender often face additional challenges when placed in detention or residential placement. Juvenile placement facilities generally do not take into consideration an adolescent's sexual orientation or gender identify. Since many facilities are not equipped or trained to address the specific needs of these children, these children are subjected to harmful practices for the convenience of the staff.

The following are the kinds of practices LGBT youth may face during their stay at a juvenile facility:[2]

- Isolation. These children are frequently placed in isolation in order "to protect them" from other residents. Isolation can mean being in a small room for twenty-three hours a day.
- Denied access to services. While in isolation these children may not be able to participate in activities with the general population.

- Experience taunts or threats from other children or from staff. LGBT youth frequently feel unsafe because staff members refuse to intervene when youth experience threats or taunts from others.
- Hygiene issues. LGBT youth may face challenges when showering, or in wearing the institution's uniform.
- Mislabeled as sex offenders because of their orientation and housed with others who have committed a sexual offense, regardless of the crime the LGBT child may have charged with.

These issues can create additional stress for LGBT youth, which can in turn lead to increased depression and anxiety.

SEXUAL ORIENTATION AS A PATHWAY INTO
THE JUVENILE JUSTICE SYSTEM

Research suggests that for LGBT children, sexual orientation may have been the pathway into the juvenile justice system. According to the Child Welfare League of America's Best Practice Guidelines for Serving LBGT Youth in Out of Home Care:

> A large proportion of LGBT youth enter [the child welfare or juvenile justice system] for reasons either directly or indirectly related to their sexual orientation or gender identify. This includes youth who . . . have been rejected, neglected or abused by their birth families; youth you have stopped attending school because of anti-LGBT abuse or harassment; runaway, "throwaway," and homeless youth, some of whom engage in survival crimes; and youth who have been mislabeled as sex offenders simply because of their sexual orientation or gender identity.

In addition, "A study of lesbian and gay youth in New York City's child welfare system found that more than half (56%) of the youth interviewed said they stayed on the streets at times because they felt safer there than living in group or foster homes."[3]

WHAT A CONCERNED ADULT CAN DO

As a concerned adult it is important for you to know the child's rights. If the court places a child in a facility, it is the state's responsibility to ensure his physical and mental well-being. The child has the right to be safe.

If the child is complaining about treatment in the facility as a result of sexual orientation, contact the program director, the child's attorney, any of the resources listed below, or the resources listed at the end of this chapter. Chapter 17 also has detailed information about what to do if you suspect institutional abuse.

NOTES

1. These facts come from the 2006 case of *R.G. v. Koller*, 415 F.Supp.2d 1129. The court found the practice of isolation to be both harmful and punitive. Ultimately, these issues were brought to the court when the child's public defender filed a petition for writ of habeas corpus.
2. Shannan Wilber, Caitlin Ryan, and Jody Marksamer, *CWLA Best Practice Guidelines, Serving LGBT Youth in Out-of-Home Care* (Washington, DC: Child Welfare League of America, 2006). For more information about this book go to www.cwla.org.
3. Wilber, Ryan, and Marksamer, *CWLA Best Practice Guidelines*, 5.

19

The Special Needs of Girls

TOP TIPS

1. Learn to de-escalate conflict.
2. Rather than focusing on the girl's behavior, try to understand what is driving the behavior.
3. Although girls are the fastest-growing population in the juvenile justice system and account for 29 percent of all juvenile arrests, the justice system was not designed with girls in mind.[1] As a result, many girls are not well served.

Everyone knew Joanne would get probation. Standing in front of the judge, admitting to a minor retail theft, all she had to do was get through a few questions and she would be out the door. But the judge irritated Joanne, making comments that she found annoying. Joanne responded by rolling her eyes and placing her hand on her hip. When the judge told her to "adjust her attitude," Joanne exploded. Telling the judge to "F—off," she immediately landed herself back in detention.

Joanne is not unusual. I have represented many young women who make their situations worse by being mouthy, defiant, and disrespectful to authority figures. I've frequently heard probation officers say they would rather have ten boys to supervise rather than one girl.

Adults dealing with teen girls are often pulled between feeling worried about the girl's safety and infuriated by the girl's outrageous words and actions. It is difficult to give love and support when she has just returned from being out all night and you've spent the night talking to the police, worried that she's been killed. It's difficult to convey how dangerous her behavior is without resorting to judging her. A parent angry about a girl's overnight disappearance might not come across as loving and relieved. Telling her "You make me so worried!" and "You make me so angry!" can further alienate an already irritable girl.

WHAT MAKES GIRLS SO ANGRY? UNDERSTANDING THE CRITICAL ROLE OF TRAUMA

Research also reveals that while all children in the juvenile justice system have higher rates of trauma than the general population, girls in the justice system have trauma rates as high as 90 percent.[2] There has been the most publicity about girls who have been traumatized by sexual and physical abuse as well as familial substance abuse and domestic violence. Of the many girls who report violence in their dating relationships, half said their partners were drunk at the time. Most girls do not tell their friends or family about dating violence. Girls can also suffer trauma from their parents' divorce, as well as loss from the death or extended absence of a parent or other close family member. Although exposure to these family problems may have occurred years before and the parent may have protected the children by becoming sober, leaving a batterer, or some other positive action, the trauma may still be affecting the girl's behavior long afterward.

To cope with trauma, girls often engage in the following behaviors:

- Self-medication with drugs or alcohol
- Self-mutilation or cutting
- Promiscuity
- Running away

It is these behaviors that often lead girls to the juvenile justice system. Because the justice system focuses on the "behaviors" of the girls, misdiagnosis frequently occurs.

Court psychological evaluations often label girls with "oppositional defiant disorder." This is a fancy name for "angry teenager."

While these girls may react especially negatively to outside controls, their aggression is often a self-defense mechanism against past abuse. The problem with the diagnosis of oppositional defiant disorder is that the trauma that leads the girl to engage in aggressive or defiant behavior goes unaddressed. The longer the trauma goes untreated, the more damaging it can become. The frustrated adult may pull away from a teen girl because of her acting out, just when she needs compassionate adults to show unconditional love.

Mistakes also occur when the court focuses solely on drug use. Girls self-medicate trauma with drugs and alcohol. A girl might believe she is using alcohol or drugs to fit in with peers and not recognize that she is numbing her anger and sadness from the past. Ordering the girl into a drug program because she smokes pot will not address the underlying reasons of why she needs to self-medicate with drugs. Depression is also common but often not diagnosed in delinquent girls. The behavioral problems rather than the underlying trauma become the court's focus.

UNDERSTANDING GIRLS' ADOLESCENT DEVELOPMENT

Girls are different than boys, and their pathways into the juvenile justice system reflect this difference. Unfortunately, research into girls' distinctive adolescent development is incomplete. The research that does exist reveals the following insights into girls' pathways toward delinquent behavior.

Low Self-Esteem

As many girls move into adolescence, they report significantly lower levels of self-competence (perceived self-worth; physical appearance; social, academic, and athletic competence) than boys, which may drive their associations with antisocial peers. Girls who previously seemed resilient become preoccupied with perfection. Some girls who once excelled stop excelling to avoid competition; some become less outspoken for fear that they will be disliked.

This drop in a girl's self-esteem can be very upsetting to concerned adults. This is particularly true for parents who have done everything they could to provide the girl with opportunities. Parents may worry about what they have done wrong. If they have divorced or have had personal problems, they may feel guilty that these have contributed to their daughter's drop in self-esteem. It is difficult to understand just how to help the girl, and, unfortunately, the adult may resort to critical sounding statements such as "What's wrong with you?" "Why are you so concerned what those girls think?" "You don't seem to be trying anymore."

School Failure

School failure is a significant risk factor for girls. The transition to middle school is an especially difficult time for girls for a lot of reasons. First, there are the obvious biological changes that occur in puberty, which may result in unfamiliar sexual attention. Second, for the first time in school, girls are moving from class to class rather than having one teacher all day. The resulting loss of a stable adult figure in the person of one all-day teacher can be particularly difficult.

In a study of the California juvenile justice system, a staggering 85 percent of the delinquent girls had been suspended or expelled at least once. Other studies have found that delinquent girls are years behind their peers academically and typically fall through the cracks in the school system.

Relationships

A key component of girls' development is the relationships and connections they develop with others. Relationships are critical, and girls in adolescence may engage in destructive behavior because of the value they place on relationships.

CASE STUDY: TIA

During her lifetime, Tia had experienced abuse and neglect.[3] Her mother had a long-standing drug problem. Her parents separated when she was young, and she lived in a lot of different places with various relatives and friends. The most stable home she remembered was a house that did not have running water, so the family would collect rainwater to wash. Other children constantly teased Tia because of her situation, and she felt friendless and inadequate. Two years before her first arrest, the house she was living in collapsed. In addition, Tia was sexually assaulted by her sister's boyfriend when she was twelve.

When Tia was fourteen she met James. She fell so in love. He was nineteen and meant everything to Tia. They had been dating for about six months when she became pregnant with his child. But Tia's sister insisted that she terminate the pregnancy, telling her that she couldn't live in the house if she had the baby. Although she wanted the baby, Tia had an abortion. A few months after the abortion, Tia met James in the local store. James told her that the relationship was over. He told her that he "heard that she was giving it out to someone else." Tia denied this, but James continued to reject her.

Moments after the breakup, Tia walked home. She said hello to her sister, then picked up a kitchen knife. She walked back to the store and plunged the knife into the jugular vein of James's neck.

Luckily, James didn't die, but Tia's first arrest was for attempted murder. Her behavior may sound crazy, irrational, and indefensible, but it makes sense in the context of the relationship. Her anger/frustration/shame at losing this relationship was more than she could handle. The extreme reaction to the end of her relationship is better understood when considering that girls who have been traumatized are often extremely vulnerable. Aggression is a common defense against the helplessness experienced by girls.

In less extreme cases, it is common for adults to wonder why a girl would become so involved with an older or otherwise inappropriate boyfriend and make so many sacrifices for the relationship. It is important to set aside adult reactions and stand in the girl's shoes to understand what is behind her tie to her boyfriend. Unless what is driving her behavior is addressed through self-acceptance and a sense of mastery from other relationships, she is unlikely to be able to avoid this or other boyfriends.

ARE GIRLS GETTING MORE VIOLENT?

Not necessarily. Some experts have found that the increase of girls in the justice system is a result of many factors, including:

- Relabeling of girls' family conflicts as violent offenses
- Changes in police practices regarding domestic violence
- Zero-tolerance policies

For example, twenty years ago, when a mother called the police because her daughter was out of control, the police officer may have just talked to the girl rather than arrest her. In addition, girl fights in school used to be dealt with by the principal's office, and now, because of zero-tolerance laws, the girl fight is likely to end up in juvenile court.

HOW DOES THE JUSTICE SYSTEM FAIL GIRLS?

It is important to remember that the juvenile system was originally created for delinquent boys: the system is just learning how to address girls' needs.

Criminalizing Abused Girls

Many girls in the justice system have been trauma victims. When a judge with good intentions finds a girl guilty in order to "get her help," the judge is giving her a criminal record, or criminalizing her behavior. As I have mentioned in other sections of this book, juvenile records do not go away when a child turns eighteen. The criminal records that girls have may follow them far into the future, undermining their potential employment opportunities.

Minor Charge Leads to Long-Term System Involvement

Although a girl may originally be arrested on a minor charge, she may stay in the system for years. Since girls come to the criminal justice system with complex needs, judges try to "fix" the problems through various types of services. Even if the girl is not rearrested on more charges, a judge can keep her in detention or extend her probation whenever she fails to comply with a court order (such as attending school or meeting curfew).[4]

For example, within a zero-tolerance school environment it is possible that a girl will be arrested on a relatively minor offense, such as shoving another girl. When she gets to court an evaluation will be done. The evaluation is likely to indicate that she has mental health issues. To address the mental health issues, the judge may first place her on probation. However, depending on her family's capacity to provide support, the availability of a counselor the girl finds helpful, the commitment of the probation officer, and other factors, the girl may not respond well to probation.

At this point, the judge will determine that she violated probation. Now the girl could be placed in a juvenile facility because of the violation. If the placement is not appropriate to her needs, she may fail to adjust at the placement. Again, the judge will see that the girl failed and may place her in a more secure facility. The cycle goes on and on. It is not uncommon for a girl to start off as a runaway or a truant and run away or stay out of school again or have only one misdemeanor arrest and stay in various types of detention for years.

Girls Who Live in Groups Tend to Do Worse

Traumatized girls are described as more difficult to work with in residential programs. Girls' behaviors worsen when they live in groups. Behavior management systems have been shown to fail with girls, but they continue to be used, and across the country disciplinary point systems do little more than antagonize girls. Girls in group care are harmed by:

- Being separated from people to whom they are attached
- Not living in a family and participating in the normalizing experience of a community school
- The uncertainty of having no permanent home

WHAT CAN A CONCERNED ADULT DO TO MEET A GIRL'S NEEDS?

Treat Her with Respect

Girls say that they are provoked by adults. Because of past trauma, they may be extremely sensitive to the abuse of power by adults and misinterpret limit setting as victimization. Many times adults will not feel that what they say or do is disrespectful, but the girl will react as if she is being mistreated. It is difficult to stand in her shoes and have her perspective.

Allow the Girl to Have Some Control Over Her Life

Traumatized girls are often more controlling than adults can tolerate. They need to be taught how to take charge without being argumentative or aggressive. Each girl must be involved with her family and professionals in designing fair, consistent methods to address conflict before it escalates.

Help Her Make Attachments

A system of services that encourages continuity of relationships is essential for girls. A girl should not be moved from place to place, which has been found to be disruptive for girls' development. Progress should not result in a move that separates her from the attachments that supported her achievements.

Teach Her How to Self-Soothe

Although they often do not recognize it, girls experience high levels of anxiety that may quickly escalate to an emotional explosion. Adults frequently react negatively to the intense emotions and behavior that are driven by the girl's anxiety. Each girl has to learn to recognize how it feels when she is starting to be anxious and how to calm herself. It is difficult to find someone who can teach a girl how to soothe herself. Self-soothing has to do with comforting and being kind to yourself. Self-soothing techniques can include the following:

Writing in a journal
Listening to music
Taking a walk or getting some other kind of exercise
Distractions such as watching a movie or a funny TV show
Cooking something that smells good
Calling a friend
Reading a magazine

Give Her Tools to Cope with Her Feelings
in the Present and the Past

Girls often exhibit a pattern of running away or using substances when they feel overwhelmed, particularly in conflict situations. Learning to face feelings from the past and in the present helps a girl change these habits. Adults who remain calm and nonreactive, who encourage her to stay safe, and who give her recognition for expressing her feelings in words support a girl in the process of making peace with the past.

Help Her Learn How to React to Threat

At an early age girls who have been traumatized learned to constantly scan their environment for possible threats, and this self-protective mechanism may cause them problems now. Small provocations may evoke explosions from a volcano of feelings left over from trauma, or girls may get angry to avoid pain from the past. Adults trying to quiet a loud girl are often misperceived as disliking her or disapproving of her outspokenness, thus antagonizing her more. She may feel she has to seek protection, even from individuals who do not support her positive development. Each girl has to learn what to do with her intense anger or fear when she feels threatened.

Teach Her to Compensate for Her Disabilities

As many as half of the girls in juvenile justice system have learning disabilities. While some have been placed in special education for emotional disturbance, they often have not had effective specialized instruction for their learning disabilities. Girls must learn how their processing and comprehension difficulties, attention problems, and organizational deficits affect them both in and out of school.

Encourage Her How to Be Physically Healthy

Psychological distress and physical health complaints are related in girls, who have higher rates of asthma, migraines, self-mutilation, and eating disorders than boys. Rates of HIV infection, pelvic inflammatory disease, HPV, precancerous and cancerous lesions, and pregnancy rates are higher than in the general population. Girls need access to health care and support to keep themselves healthy.

Praise Her Rather Than Punish Her

For years their negative behavior may have gotten more attention than when they excelled. Try to motivate the girl to change her behavior by focusing on relationships, responsibilities, and privileges rather than punishment.

Consider Counseling or a Mother-Daughter Group

It is vital for parents and their daughters to have a safe place to discuss the realities of girlhood. Going to counseling with the agenda of nurturing good communication is one option, as long as the girl does not feel she is being dragged to counseling because of her problems. There may be therapeutic support groups for girls or for parents, although often these are set up for families who are experiencing crises. A more comfortable option would be to set up a mother-daughter group with several friends and same-age daughters where each mother-daughter pair can take responsibility for kicking off a topical discussion at each meeting. These groups may end up doing activities together, including community service (such as preparing meals for homeless families), theater trips, beauty treatments, museum visits, or outdoor trips. If the goal of such a group is keeping honest, respectful, loving communication going between mothers and daughters, the self-esteem, academic, and relationship aspects of girl's development can be the source of dialogue rather than conflict. Especially if the mothers start the group proactively before there is a crisis, a self-organized group may do as much or more good than counseling.

END NOTE: NEVER GIVE UP! NEVER GIVE UP! NEVER GIVE UP!

Your girl needs you. Parenting a girl can be an enormous challenge However, for teen girls, everything is about relationships. If there has been trauma or a move away from family or friendships, a girl is likely to come back to family in the future and resume close relationships. Everything the parent has done, all the unconditional care and messages of love, encouragement, and pride in the girl the parent can muster during the difficult years provide a foundation for that return.

NOTES

The information in the section "What Can a Concerned Adult Do to Meet a Girl's Needs?" was provided by Dr. Marty Beyer and is used with her permission.

1. Howard N. Snyder and Melissa Sickmund, *Juvenile Offenders and Victims: 2006 National Report* (Washington, DC: U.S. Department of Justice, Office of Justice Programs, Office of Juvenile Justice and Delinquency Prevention, 2006).
2. Julian D. Ford, John F. Chapman, Josephine Hawks, and David Albert, "Trauma among Youth in the Juvenile Justice System: Critical Issues and New Directions," National Center for Mental Health and Juvenile Justice, June 2007, www.ncmhjj.com. See also Cathy S. Widom and Michael G. Maxfield, "An Update on the Cycle of Violence," *National Institute of Justice Research in Brief*, February 2001, www.ncjrs .gov/pdffiles1/nij/184894.pdf.
3. This topic is explored in detail based on the case experience of one girl in M. Beyer, G. Blair, S. Katz, S. Simkins, and A. Steinberg, "A Better Way to Spend $500,000: How the Juvenile Justice System Fails Girls," *Wisconsin Women's Law Journal* 18 (Spring 2003): 51–75.
4. In 1980, Congress passed an amendment to the Juvenile Justice Delinquency Prevention Act known as the "valid court order" amendment. The amendment allows juvenile judges to order detention for juveniles who violate a valid court order. 42 U.S.C. Sec. 5633(a)(12)(a)(1988).

20

When the Child Is Charged with a Sexual Offense

TOP TIPS

1. This is extremely serious. You *must* understand the long-term consequences before you agree to anything.
2. The child could face lifetime registration as a sex offender and civil commitment.
3. Make sure the child's attorney has expertise in this area. Use the questions in this chapter to test the attorney's knowledge.

Joshua is fourteen. For the past year he has been in counseling at the local sex abuse counseling center, because he was sexually abused by a cousin over the course of two years when he was younger. His grandparents took him to counseling when they noticed changes in Joshua's behavior at home and at school. Eventually, Joshua revealed to them what he had been through, and they wanted to get him help. The cousin had moved out of state and was never prosecuted.

The counselor tells Joshua that he will get the most out of his therapy if he completely opens up. After a year of seeing his therapist three times a week, Joshua reveals that before he started therapy he touched the penis of his ten-year-old male cousin and cajoled the cousin to touch Joshua's penis as well. Joshua said this happened one time and that it has not happened since. The therapist, believing himself a mandatory reporter, calls the police. Joshua is arrested for a second-degree sexual assault and faces lifetime registration as a sex offender.

• • •

Imagine your child's picture on the Internet, listed on a sexual offender registry for the rest of his or her life. This is not science fiction. Of all the ways that juvenile law has become more punitive, this is one of most frightening. Today, a child who is adjudicated delinquent on certain types of sexual offenses could face lifetime registration requirements and civil commitment. It is absolutely critical that you understand the potential consequences of any plea deals, not just the consequences for today, but how the admission may impact your child's future.

A normal part of adolescents' development is understanding their own sexuality. Adolescents are learning to think of themselves as sexual beings, to deal with sexual feelings, and to enjoy physical contact with others. Experimentation with these new feelings and sensations is normal.

However, in some of the cases that come to juvenile court, it is difficult to distinguish between normal adolescent experimentation and criminal activity. For example, if a boy and a girl, both age twelve and a half, decide to engage in consensual sexual activity, and the law says that a child under the age of thirteen is incapable of consent, should the boy be charged with rape?

Working with children charged with sexual offending is often complicated because children who are charged with sexual offenses are often victims themselves. Statistics reveal that 20 to 50 percent have a history of being physically abused and 40 to 80 percent have a history of being sexually abused. Frequently, children are charged with sexual offenses for acting out what has been done to them.

FACT VERSUS FICTION

People are afraid of sex offenders. People want to keep their children safe. Lawmakers get a lot of mileage out of supporting very harsh sexual offender laws. Unfortunately, there is a lot of misinformation about children charged with sex offenses. What is a sexual offense?

There are huge variations in sexual offenses. Lower-level offenses include:

- Indecent exposure (where a child exposes his or her genitals to another)
- Indecent assault (a boy grabs a girl's breast during science class or a girl rubs up against a boy in an elevator)
- Consensual sex with someone who is a number of years younger, also known as statutory rape

More serious offenses include:

- Rape
- Aggravated sexual assault

TABLE 20.1 Juvenile Sex Offending: Fact versus Fiction

Common misconception	Current evidence
Juvenile sex offenders will become adult sex offenders.	Studies suggest that the rates of sexual reoffense (5–14%) are substantially lower than the rates for other delinquent behavior (8–58%).[1] The assumption that the majority of juvenile sex offenders will become adult sex offenders is not supported by current literature nor valid studies.[2]
Juvenile sex offenders should be placed in secure residential treatment facilities.	Most juvenile sex offenders can safely remain in the community during treatment.[3] Decisions about placement in residential or secure settings should depend on community safety and treatment issues. The possible negative effects of out-of-home placement, such as increased risk of socialization into a delinquent lifestyle, negative peer influences, weakening of parental involvement in treatment, and disruption of normal adolescent social development, should be considered.
Juvenile sex offenders are similar in most ways to adult offenders.	Most juvenile sex offenders differ from adult sex offenders in several ways: • Adolescent sex offenders are considered to be more responsive to treatment than adult sex offenders and do not appear to continue reoffending into adulthood, especially when provided with appropriate treatment.[4] • Adolescent sex offenders have fewer numbers of victims than adult offenders and, on average, engage in less serious and aggressive behaviors.[5]

(Continued)

TABLE 20.1 Juvenile Sex Offending . . . (*Continued*)

Common misconception	Current evidence
Juvenile sex offenders are similar in most ways to adult offenders. (*continued*)	• Most adolescents do not have deviant sexual arousal and/or deviant sexual fantasies, which many adult sex offenders have.[6] • Most juveniles are not sexual predators, nor do they meet the accepted criteria for pedophilia.[7] • Few adolescents appear to have the same long-term tendencies to commit sexual offenses that some adult offenders do. • Across a number of treatment research studies, the overall sexual recidivism rate for adolescent sex offenders who receive treatment is low in most U.S. settings as compared to adults. Adolescents who offend against young children tend to have slightly lower sexual recidivism rates than adolescents who sexually offend against other teens.[8]

Source: Nicole Pitman, Esq., Juvenile Justice Policy Analyst Attorney, Defender Association of Philadelphia. Used with permission.

1. J. R. Worling and T. Curwin, "Adolescent Sexual Offender Recidivism: Success of Specialized Treatment and Implication for Risk Prediction," *Child Abuse and Neglect* 24 (2000): 965–982. D. D. Schram, D. Milloy, and W. E. Rowe, *Juvenile Sex Offenders: A Follow-Up Study of Reoffense Behavior* (Olympia, WA: Washington State Institute for Public Policy, 1991).

2. Association for the Treatment of Sexual Abusers, "The Effective Legal Management of Juvenile Sex Offenders," Position Paper, March 11, 2000 (Beaverton, OR: ATSA, 2000), http://www.atsa.com/ppjuvenile.html.

3. D. L Burton and J. Smith-Darden, The SaferSociety Foundation, *North American Survey of Sexual Abuser Treatment and Models: Summary Data* (Brandon, VT: SaferSociety Press, 2000).

4. Association for the Treatment of Sexual Abusers, "The Effective Legal Management of Juvenile Sex Offenders."

5. A. O. Miranda and C. L. Corcoran, "Comparison of Perpetration Characteristics Between Male Juvenile and Adult Sexual Offenders: Preliminary Results," *Sexual Abuse: A Journal of Research and Treatment* 12 (2000): 179–188.

6. Association for the Treatment of Sexual Abusers, "The Effective Legal Management of Juvenile Sex Offenders." Miranda and Corcoran, "Comparison of Perpetration Characteristics Between Male Juvenile and Adult Sexual Offenders."

7. American Psychiatric Association, *Diagnostic and Statistical Manual of Mental Disorders*, 4th ed. (Washington, DC: American Psychiatric Association, 1994).

8. M. A. Alexander, "Sexual Offender Treatment Efficacy Revisited," *Sexual Abuse: A Journal of Research* 11, no. 2 (1999).

WHAT DOES "CIVIL COMMITMENT"
FOR SEX OFFENDERS MEAN?

Civil commitment is a process in which a judge decides whether a person is mentally ill and should be required to go to a psychiatric hospital for an indefinite period of time. Recently, states have begun using civil commitment laws to confine juveniles who have been charged with sexual offenses, even after they complete their juvenile probation or placement. This means that even though the child may have completed his treatment program in juvenile court, he may be subject to civil commitment laws well into adulthood.

As of March 14, 2007, twenty states have civil commitment for sex offenders. Of these twenty states, eleven states civilly commit juvenile sex offenders. Pennsylvania is the only state that civilly commits juveniles but not adults. See table 20.2.

WILL THE CHILD HAVE TO REGISTER
AS A SEX OFFENDER?

If the child is found guilty (adjudicated delinquent) of a sexual offense, he may be classified as a sexual offender and required to register as a sex offender. The registration of sexual offenders is not new (think Megan's Law); however, it has only recently been applied to juveniles. Registration is a tracking system. Sex offender registries keep information about sex offenders and where they live. This allows state authorities to monitor the location of sex offenders. Much information is also placed on the Internet, so members of the public can be aware of sex offenders in their communities.

Obviously, the stigmatization and damage caused to a child by being placed on a sex offender registry is extreme. Therefore, it is really important to understand any registry requirements before a child agrees to admit to any charges.

All fifty states register adult sex offenders. Approximately thirty-five states register juveniles. In 2009 due to the newly passed Adam Walsh Act, *all* juveniles in the United States adjudicated delinquent for certain offenses will be required to register as sex offenders for life.

TABLE 20.2 Sexually Violent Predator Civil Commitment: States at a Glance

	Children face civil commitment		Children must register as sex offenders	
	YES	NO	YES	NO
Alabama		X	X	
Alaska		X		X
Arizona		X		X
Arkansas		X	X	
California	X		X	
Colorado		X	X	
Connecticut		X		X
Delaware		X	X	
District of Columbia	X		X	
Florida	X		X	
Georgia		X		X
Hawaii		X		X
Idaho		X	X	
Illinois	X		X	
Indiana		X	X	
Iowa		X	X	
Kansas		X	X	
Kentucky		X	X	
Louisiana		X	X	
Maine		X		X
Maryland		X	X	
Massachusetts	X		X	
Michigan		X	X	

TABLE 20.2 Sexually Violent ... (*Continued*)

	Children face civil commitment		Children must register as sex offenders	
	YES	NO	YES	NO
Minnesota		X	X	
Mississippi		X	X	
Missouri		X	X	
Montana		X	X	
Nebraska		X		X
Nevada		X	X	
New Hampshire	X			X
New Jersey	X		X	
New Mexico		X		X
New York		X	X	
North Carolina		X	X	
North Dakota		X	X	
Ohio		X	X	
Oklahoma		X	X	
Oregon		X	X	
Pennsylvania	X			X
Rhode Island		X	X	
Rhode Island		X	X	
South Carolina	X		X	
South Dakota		X	X	
Tennessee		X		X
Texas	X		X	
Utah		X		X

(*Continued*)

TABLE 20.2 Sexually Violent . . . (*Continued*)

	Children face civil commitment		Children must register as sex offenders	
	YES	NO	YES	NO
Vermont		X		X
Virginia		X	X	
Washington	X		X	
West Virginia		X		X
Wisconsin	X		X	
Wyoming		X		X

Source: Nicole Pitman, Esq., Juvenile Justice Policy Analyst Attorney, Defender Association of Philadelphia. Used with permission.

THE ADAM WALSH ACT AND HOW IT WILL IMPACT CHILDREN

On July 27, 2006, the Adam Walsh Child Protection and Safety Act of 2006, HR 4472, was signed into law. This law was created to establish new guidelines for placing juveniles adjudicated delinquent on both national and state sex offender registries. States have until July 27, 2009, to come into "substantial compliance" with the federal standards and stand to lose a significant amount of money if they fail to implement the new guidelines.

To Whom Will It Apply?

Any child who has been transferred to adult court will be affected. Under the Adam Walsh Act, registration will apply to any child over the age of fourteen at the time of the offense who has been adjudicated delinquent of the following offenses:

- Engaging in a sexual act with another by either force or threat of serious violence
- Engaging in a sexual act with another by rendering unconscious or involuntarily drugging the victim
- Engaging in a sexual act with a child under the age of twelve

SEXUAL OFFENSES

Note that there is an exception for consensual sexual conduct if the victim is at least thirteen years old and the offender is no more than four years older than the victim.

Under the Adam Walsh Act, How Long Will the Child Be on the Sex Offender Registry?

Children impacted by this act will likely fall into a "Tier III" offender category. This means that the child committed an offense against someone under the age of twelve. Once placed in Tier III the child will be subjected to lifetime registration and notification. According to the Adam Walsh Act, notification means registering with the designated authorities and having your information and photograph posted on a national public Web site available for all to see. A person can request to be removed from the registry after twenty-five years if there has been a clean record and successful completion of a sex offender treatment program.

What Information Will Be Available on the National Public Web Site?

If a child is required to register as a sex offender under the Adam Walsh Act, the following information will be available to the public about the child on the sex offender registry:

- Name
- Address
- Physical description
- Current photograph
- Address of school or workplace
- Text of the sex offense for which the child must register
- License plate number and description of vehicle operated[1]

The jurisdiction where the juvenile lives will likely add the following information:

- Photo of juvenile and physical description
- DNA

- Criminal history of the juvenile
- Fingerprints
- Type of offense
- Name of victim

CAN YOUR CHILD'S LAWYER PASS THIS TEST?

Given the serious, potentially lifetime consequences of being labeled a sex offender, it is critical that the child's attorney be knowledgeable and experienced. At a minimum, the child's attorney should be able to clearly explain to you and the child the following:

1. The charges against the child
2. The consequences of being adjudicated delinquent for a sexual offense in your state (for both felony and misdemeanor charges):
   - Will the child be required to register?
   - What are the current registration procedures?
   - Does your state civilly commit juveniles?
   - Will the child be able to get his record clean?
   - Are there residency restrictions? Will the family have to move if it lives within 1,000 feet of a "structure designed for use primarily by children"?
3. In addition, the attorney must have a thorough understanding about how to defend and investigate sexual offenses. For example, has the attorney
   - Reviewed the medical records?
   - Reviewed the rape kit?
   - Received information about DNA evidence?
   - Talked to witnesses?
   - Considered the relationship between the child and the victim?
   - Thought about character witnesses?
   - Checked to see if the child has a history of mental retardation, brain injury, or autism?

Finally, given the sensitive nature of the charges, it is also important the child is comfortable talking about what happened without feeling ashamed or judged.

NOTE

This chapter was prepared with the generous assistance of Nicole Pittman, Esq.

1. U.S. Department of Justice, Office of Justice Programs, "Frequently Asked Questions: The Sex Offender Registration and Notification Act (SORNA) Final Guidelines," www.ojp .usdoj.gov/smart/pdfs.faq_sorna_guidelines.pdf.

Resources

GENERAL

Juvenile Justice Project of Louisiana
1600 Oretha Castle Haley Boulevard
New Orleans, LA 70113
Phone: (504) 522-5437
Fax: (504) 522-5430
Web: http://www.jjpl.org

Juvenile Law Center
The Philadelphia Building
1315 Walnut Street, 4th floor
Philadelphia, PA 19107
Phone: (215) 625-0551
Fax: (215) 625-2808
Web: http://www.jlc.org

National Juvenile Defender Center
1350 Connecticut Avenue, NW,
    Suite 304
Washington, DC 20036
Phone: (202) 452-0010
Fax: (202) 452-1205
E-mail: inquiries@njdc.info
Web: http://www.njdc.info

Southern Center for Human Rights
83 Poplar Street, NW
Atlanta, GA 30303
Phone: (404) 688-1202
Fax: (404) 688-9440
Web: http://www.schr.org

Youth Law Center
417 Montgomery Street, Suite 900
San Francisco, CA 94101
Phone: (415) 543-3379
Fax: (415) 956-9022
Web: http://www.ylc.org

EDUCATION AND SCHOOL DISCIPLINE

Advancement Project
1730 M Street, NW, #910
Washington, DC 20036
Phone: (202) 728-9557
Fax: (202) 728-9558
Web: http://www.advancementpro-
    ject.org

Council for Exceptional Children
Phone: (703) 264-9494

End Zero Tolerance in Our Public Schools
Web: http://endzerotolerance.com

National Center on Education, Disability, and Juvenile Justice
University of Maryland
1224 Benjamin Building
College Park, MD 20742
Phone: (301) 405-6462
Fax: (301) 314-5757
Web: http://www.edjj.org

PACER Center, Champions for Children with Disabilities
8161 Normandale Boulevard
Minneapolis, MN 55437-1044
Phone: (952) 838-9000
Fax: (952) 838-0190
Web: http://www.PACER.org

Parent Training and Information Centers (PTIs) and Community Parent Resource Centers (CPRCs) Listed by State
Web: http://www.taalliance.org

HOMELESS/RUNAWAY YOUTH
National Clearinghouse on Families
   and Youth
P.O. Box 13505
Silver Spring, MD 20911-3505
Phone: (315) 608-8098
Web: http://www.ncfy.com

RACIAL AND ETHNIC MINORITY ISSUES
Asian/Pacific Islander Youth
   Violence Prevention Center

Hawaii Office:
Department of Psychiatry, University
   of Hawaii at Manoa
1441 Kapiolani Boulevard,
   Suite 1802
Honolulu, HI 96814
Phone: (808) 945-1517
Web: http://www.apiypc.org

Building Blocks for Youth
Web: http://www.
   buildingblocksforyouth.org

The W. Haywood Burns Institute for Juvenile Justice, Fairness and Equity
180 Howard Street, Suite 320
San Francisco, CA 94105
Phone: (415) 321-4100
Fax: (415) 321-4140
E-mail: info@burninstitute.org
Web: http://www.burnsinstitute.org

Center for Children's Law and Policy
417 Montgomery Street, Suite 900
San Francisco, CA 94104
Phone: (415) 543-3379
Fax: (415) 956-9022
Children's Defense Fund
Web: http://www.childrensdefense
   .org/site/PageServer?pagename
   =Programs_Cradle_Juvenile
   _Justice

National Association for the Advancement of Colored People (NAACP)
Legal Defense and Educational
   Fund Inc.
1444 I Street, NW
Washington, DC 20005
Phone: (202) 682-1300
Web: http://www.naacpldf.org

MENTAL HEALTH
National Center for Mental Health and Juvenile Justice
Policy Research Associates
345 Delaware Avenue
Delmar, NY 12054
Phone (toll-free): (866) 9NC-MHJJ
   (962-6455)
Fax: (518) 439-7612
Web: http://www.ncmhjj.com

National Mental Health Association
2001 N. Beauregard Street,
    12th floor
Alexandria, VA 22311
Phone: (703) 684-7722
Fax: (703) 684-5968
Web: http://www.nmha.org

GAY, LESBIAN, BISEXUAL, AND TRANSGENDER YOUTH

The Equity Project, a collaborative
    effort between Legal Services for
    Children, the National Center
    for Lesbian Rights, and the
    National Juvenile Defender
    Center/Lamda Legal Defense
    and Education Fund, provides
    education and tools for LGBT
    advocates.
Web: http://www.lamdalegal.org/
    cgi-bin/iowa/index.html

National Center for Lesbian Rights
870 Market Street, Suite 370
San Francisco, CA 94102
Phone: (415) 392-6527
Fax: (415) 392-8442
Web: http://www.nclrights.org

SEX OFFENSES

For additional information on the Adam Walsh Act see:
U.S Department of Justice
Office of Justice
Web: http://www.ojp.usdoj.gov/smart/
    pdfs.faq_sorna_guidelines.pdf
This document defines what sexual
    offenses are. Basically, a child
    who is fourteen or older and

commits a sexual offense faces
lifetime registration; if tried as
an adult, then SORNA (Sex
Offender Registration and
Notification Act).

LAW SCHOOL CLINICS AND CENTERS

Columbia Law School Child Advocacy Clinic
New York, NY
Phone: (212) 854-4291
Web: http://www.law.columbia.edu/
    focusareas/clinics/childadvocacy

Georgetown Law Juvenile Justice Clinic
Washington, DC
Phone: (202) 662-9100
Email: clinics@law.georgetown.edu
Web: http://www.law.georgetown
    .edu/clinics

Harvard Law School Child Advocacy Program
Cambridge, MA
Phone: (617) 496-1684
Fax: (617) 496-4947
Email: cap@law.harvard.edu
Web: http://www.law.harvard.edu/
    academics/cap/

Loyola Law School Center for Juvenile Law and Policy
Los Angeles, CA
Phone: (213) 736-1000
Fax: (213) 380-3769
Web: http://www.lls.edu/
    juvenilelaw/

**Loyola University School of Law,
Chicago CIVITAS ChildLaw Center**
Chicago, IL
Phone: (312) 915-7120
Web: http://www.luc.edu/law

**New York University School of Law
Juvenile/Criminal Defense Clinic**
New York, NY
Phone: (212) 998-6477
Web: http://www.law.nyu.edu

North Carolina Central School of Law
Durham, NC
Phone: (919) 530-6333
Web: http://nccu.edu/law

**Northwestern University Law School
Children and Family Justice Center**
Chicago, IL
Phone: (312) 503-0396
Web: http://www.law.northwestern
    .edu//cfjc

**Rutgers School of Law–Camden
Children's Justice Clinic**
217 N. 5th Street
Camden, NJ 08102
Phone: (856) 225-6425
Web: http://www.camlaw.rutgers
    .edu/site/childjustice/

**Suffolk University Law School
Juvenile Justice Center**
Boston, MA
Phone: (617) 305-3200
Fax: (617) 451-2641
Email: juvenile@suffolk.edu
Web: http://www.law.suffolk.edu/
    academic/clinical/jjc/index.cfm

**Tulane University Law School
Juvenile Litigation Clinic**
New Orleans, LA
Phone: (504) 865-5939
Fax: (504) 617-451-2641
Web: http://www.law.tulane.edu

**University of Arizona, James E.
Rogers College of Law**
Tucson, AZ
Phone: (520) 626-5232
Web: http://www.law.arizona.edu

**University of Connecticut School
of Law, KidsCounsel Center for
Child Advocacy**
65 Elizabeth Street
Hartford, CT 06105
Phone: (860) 570-5327
Fax: (860) 570-256
Web: http://www.kidscounsel.org

**University of District of Columbia,
David A. Clarke School of Law,
Juvenile and Special Education
Law**
Washington, DC
Phone: (202) 274-5073
Fax: (202) 274-5569
Web: http://www.law.udc.edu

**University of Florida Gator
TeamChild Juvenile Advocacy
Clinic**
Gainesville, FL
Phone: (352) 392-0412
Fax: (352) 392-0414
Web: http://www.law.ufl.edu/
    centers/juvenile/

University of Maryland School of
Law, Juvenile Law, Children's Issues
and Legislative Advocacy Clinic
500 W. Baltimore Street
Baltimore MD
Phone: (410) 706-7214
Web: http://www.law.umaryland.edu

University of Miami School of Law
Children and Youth Law Clinic
1311 Miller Drive, Suite F2305
Coral Gables, FL 33146
Phone: (305) 284-3123
Fax: (305) 284-4384
Web: http://www.law.miami.edu

University of Minnesota Law School
Child Advocacy Clinic
Minneapolis, MN
Phone: (612) 625-1000
Fax: (612) 625-2100
Web: http://www.law.umn.edu/
    clinics/child_advocacy.html

William S. Boyd School of Law
University of Nevada–Las Vegas
    Juvenile Justice Clinic
Las Vegas, NV
Phone: (702) 895-2080

Fax: (702) 895-2081
Web: http://www.law.unlv.edu/
    clinic_juvenileJustice.html

University of Richmond School
of Law Delinquency Clinic
Richmond, VA
Phone: (804) 289-8921
Web: http://law.richmond.edu

University of South Carolina School
of Law Children's Law Office
Columbia, SC
Phone: (803) 777-1646
Fax: (803) 777-8686
Web: http://childlaw.sc.edu/

Washburn University School of Law
Juvenile Practice
Topeka, KS
Phone: (785) 231-1191
Web: http://www.washburnlaw.edu

Yale Law School Advocacy for
Children and Youth Center
New Haven, CT
Phone: (203) 432-4800
Web: http://www.law.yale.edu

Index

Adam Walsh Act, 198
addiction. *See* drugs
ADHD (Attention Deficit
  Hyperactivity Disorder), 164.
  See also mental health
adjudication of delinquency,
  consequences of, 2. *See also*
  juvenile record
adjudicatory hearing, 12, 70, 79, 80
admitting guilt. *See* admitting to
  charges
admitting to charges, 8, 9, 12, 45,
  49; at detention hearing, 49;
  frequently asked questions
  about, 77; deciding if a child
  should, 69–71, 78; rights given
  up by, 79
adolescent development: of brain, 7,
  11; and comprehension of legal
  rights, 17, 26; in girls, 181; of
  intellectual capacity, 26; and peer
  pressure, 11; and risk taking, 11;
  and vulnerability to authority
  figures, 26; and vulnerability to
  giving false confessions, 23, 26
adult court. *See* transfer to adult
  court
adult prison, 129. *See also* transfer to
  adult court
alcohol, 180. *See also* drugs
alibi, 63, 75. *See also* defenses,
  common
anger management, 94

apologies: to court, 101; to victim,
  101
appeal, right of, 81
arrest, as parental strategy for
  behavior problem, 34
arrest warrant: child is "wanted," 31;
  getting legal advice about, 31;
  nonwaiver of rights form, 31;
  possible future warrant, 31–32;
  warrant has been issued, 32
attorney: access to, while in
  placement, 119; admitting guilt
  to, 63; appointment of, when
  child cannot afford, 45; and
  confidentiality, 63; conversations
  with, 63; recommendation of, 76;
  right to, 3, 7; role of, at pretrial
  stage, 61; role of, during transfer
  hearing, 132; working with, 8;
  work product, 64

bail, 43, 44
behavior in school, 141
bench warrant: definition of, 119;
  when child runs away from
  placement, 119. *See also* arrest
  warrant
"beyond a reasonable doubt"
  standard, 79
bind over. *See* transfer to adult court
bisexual. *See* LGBT children
bullying, 42
burden of proof, 79

About the Author

Sandra Simkins codirects the Children's Justice Clinic at Rutgers Camden School of Law. She has dedicated her career to fighting for the rights or children and spent many years as a public defender in Philadelphia.